CW01082397

ISBN: 9781314906080

Published by:
HardPress Publishing
8345 NW 66TH ST #2561
MIAMI FL 33166-2626

Email: info@hardpress.net
Web: http://www.hardpress.net

A CHRONICLE OF THE REIGN OF

CHARLES IX.

PUBLISHER'S NOTE.

Seven hundred and eighty copies of this book, as well as Fifty-two copies on fine Japanese vellum paper, printed for England and America combined. Each copy numbered as issued. Type distributed.

No. 558.

A

CHRONICLE OF THE REIGN

OF

CHARLES IX

By PROSPER MÉRIMÉE

WITH ONE HUNDRED AND TEN ENGRAVINGS ON WOOD
FROM DRAWINGS BY ÉDOUARD TOUDOUZE

NEWLY TRANSLATED INTO ENGLISH BY
GEORGE SAINTSBURY

LONDON
JOHN C. NIMMO
14, KING WILLIAM STREET, STRAND
MDCCCXC

CHISWICK PRESS :—C. WHITTINGHAM AND CO. TOOKS COURT
CHANCERY LANE

PROSPER MÉRIMÉE was born at Paris in the year 1803, being the son of, as I suppose, the "Mr. Merrimee" (*sic*) who served as a kind of patron to Hazlitt in his visit to Paris for the purpose of copying pictures in the Louvre. Mérimée received a legal education; but instead of proceeding either to the bar or to the bench, after the habit of French lawyers, he entered the public service. He was for some time attached to the Ministry of Foreign Affairs, then to that of Commerce; and finally he obtained the extremely congenial appointment of Inspector of Historic Monuments, in which he did much good work, and in connection with which he took many interesting journeys and produced some valuable monographs. In 1840 he undertook a mission to Spain, in the course of which he made acquaintance with the family of the future Empress Eugénie. This acquaintance had much influence on his future career. In 1844 he became a member of the French Academy. At the time of the somewhat famous Libri affair, he defended Libri, who was his friend, from the charge of abstracting public property from libraries, with such warmth, that he was prosecuted and condemned to fine and imprisonment. After the establishment of the Empire he was made a Senator (insisting with rather uncommon disinterestedness on giving up the emoluments of his former appointment).

and became one of the most intimate friends of the Imperial
household.   He made frequent visits to England, where
he had many friends, especially Mr. Ellice of Glengarry,
and Mr. (afterwards Sir Antonio) Panizzi of the British
Museum.   He had some English blood in his veins, and
was, as the mottoes of the following book will show, inti-
mately acquainted with English literature, as he was also
with Spanish, and in the later years of his life with Russian.
After middle age his health broke down, and he died
at Cannes, in October, 1870, having lived long enough to
see the downfall of the Empire and the misfortunes of
France.   It was not till after his death that a new side of
his literary talent, which had already been established in
various departments for nearly half a century, was revealed
—together with a new side of his character—to the public
by the successive publication of two large collections of
letters ; one, " À une Inconnue," and another to his friend
Panizzi.   A third collection, " À une autre Inconnue," has
less interest.   These letters, besides presenting perhaps the
best examples of epistolary style and the most various
subjects of interest to be found in any similar books since
the early years of the century, throw the fullest light on
Mérimée's curious nature.   He had been regarded in his
lifetime as a confirmed cynic, and cynicism was not wanting
in these letters ; but they also exhibited some, at least, of
the sterling qualities which underlay this mask.   Perhaps
the least favourable points in Mérimée's character were his
ostentatious parade of Freethinking and his disregard of
conventional decency ; faults which appear to some extent
in his writings, but which are said to have been much more
marked in his conversation.   Tradition assigns part, at
least, of the cause of this to some early disappointment or

deception, and a further part to the influence of Stendhal (Henri Beyle), who was a friend of Mérimée's youth, and who undoubtedly had some ascendancy over him.

Mérimée's literary work—all of which is distinguished by the presence of what good judges have regarded as the best French prose style of the century, as well as by other remarkable qualities—is both extensive and various. Although an extremely careful and accurate worker, a man of many distractions, and somewhat of a man of pleasure, he found time to produce more than a score of volumes of original and translated work of the highest literary merit. He began rather characteristically with two audacious fabrications, intended to catch the taste and tone of the then (1825) young Romantic movement. One was entitled the " Théâtre de Clara Gazul," a pretended collection of translated Spanish plays; and the other was " La Guzla," a prose collection of (equally pretended) translations of Illyrian folk-songs. Then he tried—in the work which is now presented to the reader, and in " La Jacquerie"—a variety of French romance, based on the novels of Sir Walter Scott, which he himself soon abandoned, but which was afterwards followed out with immense success by Dumas and others. Relinquishing this also, he confined himself for the rest of his life, as far as fiction was concerned, to shorter tales, the secret of which he never lost, and which constitute by far the most remarkable collection of the kind in literature. " Colomba," " Carmen," " Arsène Guillot," " La Vénus d'Ille," " Mateo Falcone," " L'Enlèvement de la Redoute," " Lokis," " La Chambre Bleue," and others, present the widest diversity of style and subject; yet every one may be called a masterpiece. No one of Mérimée's contemporaries and rivals in this art, except Théophile

Gautier, could match him in style; while he excelled Gautier
in dramatic conception of story, in close observation of life,
and in particular in the rigid exclusion of anything like
unnecessary description or digression of any kind. It is
possible that he carried this fancy for compression too
far for long stories; and a severe criticism might desire
some expansion in the present instance. But in shorter
stories the defect, if defect it be, is naturally not felt, and
the astonishing vividness which results from the quality is
felt without drawback. Although Mérimée's love-scenes
were almost always tinged with a certain cynicism, which
prevented him from attaining the exquisite Romantic beauty
of Gautier's " Morte Amoureuse," he is in all other respects
unsurpassed. " La Vénus d'Ille " and " Lokis " in the direction of supernatural horror; " L'Enlèvement de la Redoute "
in that of vivid yet chastened description of action; " Colomba," " Matéo Falcone," and " Carmen," in the fixing of
romantic national character; " Arsène Guillot " and " La
Chambre Bleue," in two different forms—the lighter and
more satiric, the more pathetic and sentimental, respec-
tively—of the old French *conte*, or story of dubious morality:
all these stand so far above their competitors, that it is
difficult to conceive their ever being equalled.

Mérimée's work in other directions to a great extent
conditioned his work in pure literature. He did not attempt
very much criticism, strictly so called; but he was a master
of the short biographical and critical notice; and he was
much addicted to historical studies, especially in Roman,
Spanish, and Russian history. He also, as has been said,
translated not a little; his practice in this respect, no doubt,
affecting his wonderfully flexible and yet wonderfully
precise and accurate style, which stands at an equal distance

from the loose opulence of Romantic colour and the somewhat jejune mathematics of Classical proportion.

It is very interesting to see how these qualities appear, even in such early work as the following book, which was written when the author was scarcely five-and-twenty. And it is also interesting to compare it with the work—" La Reine Margot"—of Dumas, written years afterwards on the same subject, and with pretty distinct indebtedness to this very book. In some respects Mérimée's work shows defect. It is doubtful whether he could ever have written a long novel or romance, his very faculty of managing the *nouvelle* or short story being rather a snare to him in this way. It is open to anyone who likes to say that the earlier chapters of this *chronique* are rather too much isolated studies of particular characteristics of the period, that their very titles stamp them as such, and that sufficient pains are not taken to melt and incorporate these studies—of a duel, of an introduction at Court, of the Renaissance combination of devotion and libertinage, of the Renaissance fancy for white, and sometimes not so very white magic—into a harmonious whole ; that Mergy is too much of the abstract *jeune premier*, Diane too little of a distinct and individual figure. Some truth must be allowed to these complaints ; but not too much. It is perfectly true that, with the exception of the pathetic-ironic figure of George de Mergy (one of the innumerable, and it would seem inevitable, instances of the need which the novelist feels of sketching himself), and perhaps of Captain Dietrich Hornstein, who owes something to Captain Dugald Dalgetty, it is more difficult than it should be to take a direct personal interest in the characters. Only in the great scene between Diane and Mergy, when the massacre has actually broken out, does the heroine become thoroughly alive ; but then she is admirable. The portrait, historic rather than fictitious, of La Noue, in the later chapters, is quite masterly ; but Charles himself is rather a shadow, and the Admiral does not by any means stand out from the canvas as he might do. The deathbed scene of George and Béville is unduly prolonged, and shows something of that deliberate and not too well-bred desire to shock orthodox notions of malice prepense, which was one of Mérimée's greatest faults. But when deductions for all this are made, how much is left ! The cabaret scene of the opening, with the gracious if naughty figure of Mila for centre, is as well conceived as anything in Dumas himself, and far better written. In the succeeding chapters something of a want of sustained interest, something of the already noticed effect of a succession of "studies," may be noticed ; but the interest gathers as it proceeds. The love-scenes (*exceptis*, yet once more *excipiendis*) not only attract in themselves, but possess the curious interest of having served as models to thousands of the same kind since, while Mérimée had hardly a model before him. And from the moment that the massacre is first seen or felt in the distance, there are few weak pages. The preliminaries—the rescue of Mergy from the mob by the jovial preaching friar, and the fruitless effort of George to keep his troopers' hands free from murder—are excellent ; and even if the actual description of the massacre were not associated with the fine scene between Diane and Mergy already noticed, the power and graphic force (without any fine writing or flux of epithets) of the description could not escape notice. The second cabaret scene, that of the two monks, is equal to the first, and the brief Rochelle period is a series of vignettes of the highest excellence, crowned by the more elaborate battle-piece of the capture

of the mill, which comes not far short of Mérimée's own
" Capture of the Redoubt," and probably served as model to
the one unquestionably good thing that M. Zola has done,
" L'Attaque du Moulin." In these scenes, as in the con-
cluding one which has been already criticised, the touch of
hardness, of a sort of complaisant dallying with horrible
detail, which is still more characteristic of the " Jacquerie,"
and which always more or less distinguished Mérimée as a
writer, may be a little apparent. But it certainly does not
appear sufficiently to interfere with the enjoyment of what,
if it is not the best historical novel, is probably the best
series of historico-fictitious pictures in words that French
has to show.

Nor should it be omitted that even here, early as the work
is, and comparatively imperfect as is the writer's afterwards
consummate mastery of his implements, there appears very
much of that literary and moral idiosyncrasy which makes
Mérimée so interesting a figure. There appears also that
ironic-pathetic view of life which is from first to last present
in his books, but the standpoint of which was never fully
revealed till the publication of his letters, including that very
interesting selection to Mrs. Senior and others which Count
D'Haussonville printed only the other day. Two of the
stories, remembered or invented as he wrote for the benefit
of his correspondents, which this last selection gives, are so
invaluable for providing the reader with spectacles through
which to read Mérimée, that I may perhaps be pardoned for
translating them here. This is the first :—

" Once upon a time there was a madman who thought
that he possessed the Queen of China (I need not tell you
that she is the loveliest princess in the world) shut up in a
bottle. This possession made him very happy, and he was

never tired of exerting himself, that the bottle and its inhabitant might have no reason to be ashamed of him. But one day he broke the bottle, and as one cannot hope to hit upon a Princess of China twice in one's life, he, who had only been mad before, became stupid." And here is the other :—

" Well then, when I was young, I was, as I thought, sole master of a remarkably beautiful leg—not a common thing, for reasons which I need not tire you by discussing. I had for a long time never seen it except clad in a silk stocking ; but by unwearying instances I obtained the favour of having this stocking taken off. Now the garter had left a red mark, with patches of blue-black—a mark explicable of course as a symptom of the delicacy of the skin, but still ugly. I never saw the leg afterwards without seeing the mark through the stocking."

These two stories should always be remembered, intelligently and compassionately, in reading Mérimée. But it should be remembered also that he never " posed " in society as a disappointed or blighted being. His pose, if any, was rather the other way. Even in this book, purely historical as it is for the most part, there will be found, not Byronism, though it was written in the very high tide and spring-time of that influence, but a sincerity of disillusion and disappointment, of which Byronism was generally a mere travestie. Although few good judges have refused him their admiration, a full and just literary estimate of Mérimée is still to be made ; and the latest competitor, Count D'Haussonville already mentioned, has partly eschewed the task of deliberation, partly shown that he is not quite alive to all sides of Mérimée's excellence. But we owe him, I think, the best remark yet made on Mérimée's character, the

remark that at least in later life he was dominated by and
occasionally showed " le sentiment qu'il était mal compris,
mal jugé, mais qu'il était un peu responsable de cette
injustice, et qu'il devait s'en prendre surtout à lui-même,
non seulement si on pensait quelque mal de lui, mais encore
s'il ne valait peut-être pas tout ce qu'il aurait pu valoir."
As an ethical criticism this is, I think, very acute and very
just ; but on the literary side, Mérimée scarcely *aurait pu
valoir* more than he does. His variety of interests, his fas-
tidiousness of taste, his freedom from any need of working
for a living, and his contempt of popular applause and
popular estimates, would probably, when taken together,
have always prevented him from writing a " Decline and
Fall " or an " Esprit des Lois." But he has done the very
best things of their kind in more kinds, or more subdivisions
of a kind, than one or two, and of how many men is it
possible to say that ? In this particular book, if he did not
do one of the very best things in its particular kind, he
showed a whole nation the way, which was promptly and
profitably followed, and himself turned out work of a rare
excellence.

GEORGE SAINTSBURY.

*NOTE OR POSTSCRIPT. I believe that an English transla-
tion of the " Chronique de Charles IX." has already appeared
some forty years ago : but I have never seen it, and the
demerits of the following version, such as they are, are all
my own. It would have been impossible to choose a pleasanter
relief and variation to the usual inquiry, " What the Swede
intends and what the French," and the other customary occupations of journalism : and I can only hope that the result of
the exercise is not so very much less well performed than it*

was pleasant in the performance. Mérimée, who followed Scott pretty closely, in some ways, does not appear to have aimed at much archaism of style, though he has touches of it here and there. So that if my own practice in this respect seems a little inconsistent, I may plead the desire (which indeed has been my chief desire throughout) to follow my original as closely as possible. The author himself added notes with tolerable liberality, and it seemed unnecessary to increase their number much. Indeed such additions could have served little purpose, except to apologize for the occasional substitution of one idiom for another—an apology usually as superfluous as the substitution itself is necessary. If anyone solemnly and dictionary-in-hand assures me that "à trois poils" means "three-piled," and that I have not in its particular place so translated it, I can only admit with equal solemnity that he is quite right.

CONTENTS.

CONTENTS.

AUTHOR'S PREFACE.

I HAD been reading a considerable number of memoirs and pamphlets relating to the end of the sixteenth century. I took a fancy to extract some of the matter of my reading; and the result of the process is the present book.

Anecdotes are the only part of history that I love; and among anecdotes I prefer those where it seems to me that I find a true picture of manners and character at a given time. This is not a very dignified taste; but I confess to my shame that I would willingly give Thucydides for some authentic memoirs by Aspasia or by a slave of Pericles. For

memoirs alone, which are as it were familiar conversations
of an author with his reader, furnish those portraits of human
beings which amuse and interest me.   To form an idea of
the Frenchman of the sixteenth century you must go, not to
Mézeray, but to Montluc, Brantôme, D'Aubigné, Tavannes,
La Noue, and their likes.   The very style of these contemporary authors teaches as much as their matter.

For instance, I read in L'Estoile this short note :—

" The damsel of Châteauneuf, one of the king's favourites
before he went to Poland, having married for love a certain
Florentine officer of the galleys at Marseilles, named Anti-
notti, and finding him in the act of infidelity, slew him,
manlike, with her own hands."

By dint of this anecdote, and of many others whereof
Brantôme is full, I can reconstruct a whole character in my
mind, and I can bring to life again a lady of the Court of
Henri III.

To my fancy, it is curious to compare these manners with
ours, and to note in the latter the decadence of vigorous
passions.   Hence, no doubt, a gain in quiet living, and perhaps in happiness.   But we have still to find out whether
we are better men than our ancestors ; and this question is
not so easy to settle, for ideas have greatly varied at different times on the subject of the same actions.   Thus, about
1500, a murder by dagger or poison inspired nothing like the
horror that it does now.   A gentleman killed his enemy
treacherously ; he sued for pardon, obtained it, and appeared
in society without anyone dreaming of frowning on him.
Sometimes, indeed, when the murderer had a legitimate
grievance, men spoke of him as they speak now of a man of
honour who has, in a duel, killed some scoundrel by whom
he has been grievously offended.

Thus it seems to me clear that we must not use our nineteenth century ideas in judging sixteenth century conduct. What is criminal in a state of advanced civilization is only a bold deed in a state more backward, and in a state of barbarism may perhaps be a laudable action. It is generally felt that the judgment which is passed on the same action must vary with countries as well as with times, for between nation and nation there is at least as much difference as between century and century.[1] Mehemet Ali, with whom the Mameluke Beys vied for the control of Egypt, one day invites the principal chiefs of this militia to a festival within his palace walls; when they are inside the gates are shut; Arnauts shoot them down from behind cover on the top of the courtyard walls, and from that time Mehemet Ali reigns alone in Egypt. Well, we negotiate with Mehemet Ali; Europeans even think very highly of him; he is held a great man by all the newspapers; they call him Egypt's benefactor. And yet what can be more horrible than to butcher defenceless men in this way? As a fact, murderous traps of this kind are sanctioned by the custom of the country, and by the impossibility of managing matters otherwise. 'Tis then that the maxim of Figaro, *Ma per Dio, l'utilità,* comes in. If a minister whom I will not name had found Arnauts ready to shoot at his orders, and if at a state dinner he had despatched the chief members of the Left, the action would have been, as far as actual fact went, the same as that of the Pasha of Egypt, but morally it would have been a hundred times more blameworthy. Yet this minister turned into the streets many Liberal electors

---

[1] May not this rule be extended to individuals? Is the son of a thief, who himself thieves, as culpable as an educated man who goes through a fraudulent bankruptcy?

B

who were small government functionaries, frightened the
rest, and made the elections go as he wished. If Mehemet
Ali had been a French minister he also would have taken
no stronger measures, and in the same way the French
minister would doubtless, in Egypt, have been obliged to
take to the fusillade, turnings out of office not being calcu-
lated to produce a sufficient moral effect on Mamelukes.[1]

The massacre of St. Bartholomew was a great crime even
for its own day; but, I repeat, a massacre as such in the sixteenth century was not the same crime as a massacre in the
nineteenth. Let us add that the greater part of the nation took
a share in it or sympathized with it, and armed in a body
to attack the Huguenots, who were held to be strangers and
enemies. St. Bartholomew was, in short, a national up-
rising, like that of the Spaniards in 1809; and the citizens
of Paris, when they cut the throats of the heretics, had a firm
belief that they were obeying the voice of heaven.

It is no part of the business of a teller of tales like myself
to give in this volume a *précis* of the historical incidents of
1572, but as I have mentioned St. Bartholomew I cannot
refrain from setting forth certain thoughts that have occurred
to me as I read this bloody page of our history. Have the
causes which brought about the massacre been well understood? Was it long premeditated, or was it not rather the
result of a sudden resolve, even of a chance? No historian
supplies me with satisfactory answers to any of these
questions. They all admit as evidence mere street rumours
and alleged conversations, of very small weight in deciding a
historical question of such importance. Some of them
represent Charles IX. as a prodigy of dissimulation; others
as a man of hasty, violent, and fantastic temper. If, long

[1] This preface was written in 1829.

before the 24th of August, he broke out into threats against the Protestants, it is a proof that he had long been meditating their destruction ; if he paid attentions to them, it is a proof that he was dissembling. I will quote a single story only, one repeated in all the books, and one which shows with what levity the most improbable rumours are admitted.

About a year before St. Bartholomew's Day, it is said, a plan of massacre had been already arranged ; it was this. There was to be built on the Pré-aux-Clercs a wooden tower ; the Duke of Guise, with a body of Catholic gentry and soldiery, was to be posted therein, and the Admiral with his Protestants was to have made a sham attack, as if to give the King a siege in spectacle. As soon as this kind of tournament had begun, the Catholics were, at a signal, to load their pieces and kill their surprised enemies before they could possibly stand on their guard. To improve the story, it is added that a favourite of Charles IX., named Lignerolles, foolishly revealed the plot by saying to the King, who was using harsh language about the Protestant lords, " Ah ! Sire, wait a little longer ; we have a fort which will avenge us of all the heretics " (observe, if you please, that not a stick of this fort was yet in position) ; whereupon the King took care to have the blabber assassinated. The plan, they say, was devised by the Chancellor Birague, in whose mouth, however, a saying is put which points to quite different projects—the saying, that in order to deliver the King from his enemies he wanted only a few cooks. This last method was much more practical than the other, which is so wild as to be nearly impossible. How, indeed, could the suspicions of the Protestants fail to be aroused by the preparations for this mimic war, where the two parties, open enemies just before, were to be set at one another's throats ?

while it was but an awkward way of making the Huguenots an easy prey to brigade them together and put arms in their hands. Clearly, if the idea was to exterminate them then, it would have been much better to attack them in detail and disarmed.

But for my part I have a strong conviction that the massacre was not premeditated, and I cannot conceive how the opposite opinion has been adopted by authors who at the same time concur in representing Catherine as a very wicked woman no doubt, but also as possessing one of the most statesmanlike heads of the century. Let us put morals aside for a moment, and examine the supposed design from the point of view of expediency. Now, I hold that it was not expedient for the Court ; and, moreover, that it was so bung- lingly carried out as to necessitate the supposition that those who devised it were the most reckless of mankind. Let any- one ask himself whether the King's authority had to gain or lose by this execution, and whether it was the King's interest to permit it. France was divided into three great parties : that of the Protestants, of which, since the death of Condé, the Admiral was the head ; that of the King (the weakest), and that of the Guises and the ultra-royalists of the day. It is clear that the King, to whom the Guises and the Protestants were equally objects of fear, was bound to seek to uphold his own authority by keeping these two parties at logger- heads. To crush one was to put himself at the mercy of the other. Besides, the see-saw plan was already well known. Louis XI. had said, " Divide in order to reign."

And now let us see whether Charles IX. was pious ; for excessive piety might have suggested to him steps contrary to his interest. But all evidence goes to show the reverse ; to show that, if he was not a freethinker, he was at the same time by no means a fanatic. Besides, his mother, who governed him, would never have hesitated to sacrifice her religious scruples, if she had any, to her love of power.[1]

But let us suppose that Charles, or his mother, or if any-one prefers it, his government, had in the teeth of all the principles of statecraft resolved to destroy the Protestants of France. In that case, when the resolve was once formed, it is probable that they would have given mature consideration to the means most proper for assuring success. Now one thing suggests itself at once, as essential to safety, to wit, that the massacre should take place in all the towns of the kingdom at the same time, so that the reformers, everywhere attacked by superior forces,[2] might be every-where unable to defend themselves. A single day would have been enough for their destruction ; and it was thus that Ahasuerus planned the massacre of the Jews. Yet we read that the first royal orders for massacring the Pro-testants are dated August 28th, that is to say, four days *after* St. Bartholomew, and when the news of that great butchery must have got the start of the royal despatches and have alarmed all those of " the religion."

Again, it would have been especially necessary to seize the strongholds of the Protestants ; for while they retained

[1] A saying of Charles IX. has been quoted, as an instance of profound dissimulation, which seems to me to be, on the contrary, only the coarse sally of a man quite indifferent to religion. The Pope made a difficulty of giving the necessary dispensation for the marriage of Marguerite de Valois, sister of Charles IX., with Henri IV., who was then a Protestant. " If the Holy Father refuses," said the King, " I will tuck sister Margoton under my arm and take her to be married in full meeting-house."

[2] The population of France was about twenty million souls. It was cal-culated that at the time of the second civil war the Protestants were not more than a million and a half strong ; but they were proportionally stronger in wealth, warriors, and generals.

control of these the royal authority was not assured. Thus, supposing a regular plot on the part of the Catholics to have existed, it is clear that one of the most important steps would have been to seize Rochelle by the 24th of August, and to have an army simultaneously on foot in the south of France to prevent any combined rising of the reformers.[1]

Nothing of this sort was done ; and I cannot admit that the same men were likely at once to conceive a crime the results of which must have been so momentous, and to execute it so ill. So badly indeed were measures taken, that a few months after St. Bartholomew the war broke out afresh, a war wherein the reformers won all the credit, and from which they even obtained new and solid advantage.

Lastly, does not the attempt to assassinate Coligny, which was made two days before St. Bartholomew, put the final touch to the refutation of the supposed general scheme ? Why kill the chief before the general massacre ? Was it not the very way to scare the Huguenots, and to force them to stand on their guard ?

I know that some authors attribute this attack on the Admiral's person to Guise alone : but, not to mention that public opinion accused the King of the deed,[2] and that the would-be assassin received a formal royal recompense, I should draw from the very fact of the outrage an argument against the plot. Had it really existed, the Duke of Guise must have had a hand in it ; and, if so, why not delay his private vengeance for a couple of days, so as to make its success certain ? Why risk the failure of the whole enter-

---

[1] During the second civil war the Protestants in a single day surprised more than half the fortresses of France. The Catholics could have done the same.

[2] Maurevel was surnamed "The King's Butcher." See Brantôme.

prise in the sole hope of hastening his enemy's death by forty-eight hours ?

Thus all evidence seems to me to show that this great massacre was not the result of a conspiracy on the part of the King against a section of his people. The massacre of St. Bartholomew appears to me the result of a popular rising which could not be foreseen, and which was in fact improvised ; and I shall now, in all humility, give my own explanation of the riddle.

Coligny had thrice negotiated with his sovereign on equal terms, and that was reason enough why the King should hate him. After the death of Jeanne D'Albret, the two young princes (the King of Navarre and the Prince of Condé) being too young to exercise any influence, Coligny was, in truth and in fact, the only chief of the reformed party. When he was out of the way the two princes, in their enemy's camp, and quasi-prisoners there, were at the King's mercy. Thus the death of Coligny, and of Coligny only, was important for assuring the authority of Charles, who had perhaps not forgotten the saying of the Duke of Alva, " A salmon's head is worth more than ten thousand frogs."

But if the King could get rid at once of the Admiral and of Guise, he would clearly become absolute master. The course therefore that he ought to have taken was this : to get the Admiral assassinated, or, if anyone prefers it, to suggest the assassination to the Duke of Guise, and then to have Guise himself prosecuted as a murderer, making pro-clamation that the Duke was abandoned to the vengeance of the Huguenots. It is known that Guise, whether guilty or not of Maurevel's attempt, quitted Paris in a hurry, and that the reformers, with the apparent sanction of the King, set no bounds to their threats against the princes of the House of Lorraine.

Now at this time the populace of Paris was terribly fanatical. The citizens, in their trained bands, formed a kind of national guard, ready to take arms at the first sound of the tocsin. The Huguenots, who had twice besieged the town, were as much hated as the Duke of Guise, for his own merits and his father's memory, was beloved. The kind of favour which the reformers, at the moment of the marriage of the King's sister to a prince of their faith, enjoyed at Court redoubled their own arrogance and the hatred of their enemies. In short, there was but need of a chief to put himself at the head of these fanatics, and cry " Strike ! " to make them rush at the throats of their heretical countrymen. The Duke, too, banished from Court, threatened by the King and by the Protestants, had perforce to seek support from the people. He gathers the train-band chiefs, talks to them of a plot of the heretics, bids them exterminate the plotters before their plot is ripe, and then, and then only, the massacre is meditated. As a few hours only passed between plan and execution, the mystery which surrounded the conspiracy and the keeping of the secret by so large a number of men is easily explained—a matter which otherwise seems very extraordinary, for " secrets travel fast in Paris."[1]

It is not easy to decide what part the King took in the massacre ; but if he did not approve it beforehand, he did not interfere with it. After two days of murder and outrage he disavowed the whole thing and tried to stop the carnage.[2] But the rage of the people had been let loose, and the

[1] A saying of Napoleon.
[2] He attributed the attempt on Coligny and the massacre to the Duke of Guise and the princes of the House of Lorraine.

people's thirst is not slaked with a little blood. More than sixty thousand victims were called for, and the King was obliged to swim with the resistless stream. He revoked his orders of mercy, and soon gave fresh ones for extending assassination all over France.

Such is my opinion about the massacre of St. Bartholomew; and in setting it forth I shall say with Lord Byron:

> "I only say, suppose this supposition."
>
> *Don Juan*, cant. i. stan. 85.

1829.

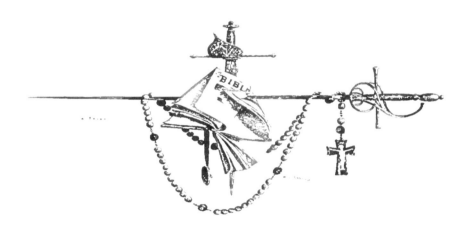

CHAPTER I.

THE REITERS.

" The black bands came over
The Alps and their snow ;
With Bourbon, the Rover,
They passed the broad Po."
LORD BYRON, *The Deformed
Transformed.*

N OT far from Étampes,
on the Paris road, there
is still to be seen a
large square building
with pointed windows
roughly sculptured.
Above the gate is a

niche where was once a stone image of Our Lady, but in
the Revolution this shared the fate of many saints of both
sexes, and was solemnly demolished by the president of the
revolutionary club of Larcy. They have since put in its
place another Virgin, which is no doubt only plaster, but
which, with a scrap or two of silk and some glass beads,
plays the part fairly well, and gives an almost venerable
air to Claude Giraut's cabaret.

More than two centuries ago, to wit, in 1572, the function
of this building was, as now, to receive thirsty travellers;
but at that time its appearance was altogether different.
The walls were covered with inscriptions bearing witness to
the varying incidents of a civil war. By the side of " Long
Live the Prince !"[1] you read " Long Live the Duke of Guise
—Death to the Huguenots !" A little further a soldier had
drawn with charcoal a gallows and its burden, adding below,
for fear of mistakes, the inscription, " Gaspard de Châtillon."
Yet it would appear that the Protestants had later had the
upper hand in these quarters, for the name of their chief had
been struck out and replaced by that of Guise. Other
legends, half rubbed out, difficult to read, and still more
difficult to translate decorously, showed that the King and
his mother had met with no more respect than these par-
tisan chiefs. But the poor Madonna herself seemed to have
had most to suffer from political and religious frenzy. The
statue, chipped by bullets in twenty places, proved the zeal
of the Huguenot soldiery in defacing what they were
pleased to call heathen images. While the pious Catholic
doffed his bonnet in veneration when passing the statue, the
Protestant trooper thought it his duty to let fly his arquebuss at it ; and if he hit he plumed himself as much as if he

----

[1] The Prince of Condé.

had brought down the Beast of the Revelations and abolished idolatry.

For some months past there had been peace between the rival sects; but the lips and not the heart had sworn it. The hatred of the factions was maintained in all its implacability. Everywhere there was a reminder that war had hardly ceased, and a promise that peace would be of no long duration. The Lion d'Or was full of soldiers. They were easily known, by their foreign accent and outlandish costume, for those German troopers known as Reiters,[1] who were in the habit of offering their services to the Protestant party, especially when the Protestant party was in case to pay them well. If skill in horsemanship and dexterity in using firearms made these strangers formidable on the day of battle, they were on the other hand renowned, and perhaps with still more justice, as accomplished plunderers, and for their ruthlessness in the hour of victory. The squadron which had taken up its quarters in the inn numbered fifty horsemen, who had left Paris the night before, and were on their way to join the garrison of Orleans.

While some of them groomed their horses fastened to the wall, others made up the fire, turned the spits, and generally attended to the cooking. The unfortunate innkeeper, cap in hand and tears in eye, gazed on the racket which was going on in his kitchen. He saw the poultry yard emptied, the cellar under contribution, bottles broken short off at the neck to save the trouble of drawing the cork, and, worst of all, he knew that, for all the King's strict ordinances as to discipline in the army, there was not the slightest compensation to expect from those who were treating him as if they were in a conquered country. It was an established principle in

[1] By corruption from the German *reuter*, 'horseman.' [In French *reître.*]

these unlucky times that, in peace or in war, armed men did
what was right in their own eyes wherever they found themselves.

Before a table of oak, blackened by grease and smoke,
sat the captain of the Reiters.
He was a tall and stout man of
about fifty, with a hooked nose
and a high colour. His scanty
and grizzled hair scarcely covered
a huge scar which began at the
left ear and lost itself in a thick
moustache. He had taken off his
helm and his cuirass, and wore
only a jerkin of Hungarian leather,
stained by the friction of his
armour, and carefully patched in
divers places. His sabre and
his pistols lay on a
bench within reach ; but
he kept his large dagger,
a weapon which no pru-
dent man then discarded
till he went to bed. At his
left sat a young man, bright-
complexioned, tall, and well-made
enough. His doublet was embroidered, and the whole of his
dress was more careful than the captain's. He was,
however, only a cornet.

Two girls of some twenty or twenty-five years kept them
company at table. Their garments, evidently not made
for them, and gained by chance of war, showed a mixture of

shabbiness and luxury. One was dressed in a kind of bodice
of damask brocaded with gold, but this bodice was tarnished,
and completed only by a skirt of plain cloth. The other
had a gown of violet velvet, and a man's hat of grey felt
adorned with a cock's feather. Both were pretty; but their
bold glances and free talk showed the results of their
association with soldiers. The functions which they left
Germany to discharge were a little uncertain. Velvet-gown
was a gipsy: she could tell fortunes with cards and play the
mandolin. The other had some knowledge of leech-craft,
and appeared to be high in the cornet's good graces. The
quartet, each with a large bottle and a glass before him or
her, chatted and drank together while waiting for their
dinner.

The conversation, as was natural between very hungry
people, was not lively at the moment that a young man of
lofty stature and dressed with some elegance halted his
good chestnut horse before the inn door. The trumpeter of
the Reiters rose from a bench where he sat, and coming
towards the stranger took his bridle. The stranger was
about to thank him for his supposed courtesy, but he was
soon undeceived. The trumpeter opened the horse's mouth,
examined his teeth like an expert, and then, stepping back
and surveying the noble animal's legs and croup, shook his
head with an air of satisfaction. "You have a good horse
between your legs, sir," he said in his jargon, and added in
German certain words which made his comrades laugh as
he returned and took his seat among them.

This cool examination did not please the traveller; but
he contented himself with a contemptuous glance at the
trumpeter, and dismounted without the aid of anyone.
The host, however, who was just stepping out, took the

bridle from his hands respectfully, and whispered sufficiently low for the Reiters not to hear, "God be your
speed, young sir, but you come at an evil chance; for the
company of these heretics (may St. Christopher wring
their necks!) is not agreeable to good Christians like you
and me."

The young man smiled bitterly. "Are these gentlemen,"
said he, "Protestant troopers?"

"Yes, and Reiters as well," quoth the host. "Our Lady
confound them! they have been here but an hour, and they
have broken half my gear. They are all pitiless plunderers, like that devil's Admiral, their fine chief, M. de
Châtillon."

"For a greybeard," answered the young man, "you are
not prudent. If perchance he to whom you spoke were a
Protestant, he might give you a broken head for an answer."
And he slashed his white leather boot with his horsewhip
as he spoke.

"How? what? You a Huguenot—a Protestant, I mean!"
cried the astounded host. He stepped back and stared
at the stranger from head to foot, as if to discover in his
dress some symptom of his religion. This scrutiny and the
open laughing countenance of the young man reassured him
a little, and he began again in a lower tone, "A Protestant
with a green velvet coat! A Huguenot with a Spanish
ruff! Impossible, my good young lord. Heretics go not
so brave. St. Mary! a velvet doublet is too fine for the
dirty varlets."

The whip whistled through the air at once, and striking
the poor Boniface across the cheek, gave him as it were his
guest's confession of faith.

"Here, insolent chatterer, is something to teach you to

keep your tongue in order. Come, take my horse to the stable, and see that he lacks naught."

The innkeeper hung his head sadly, and led the horse under a kind of shed, muttering a thousand curses against heretics, German and French alike; and had not the young man followed him to see how his horse was

treated, the poor beast would no doubt have been docked of his supper as a misbeliever.

The stranger next entered the kitchen and greeted the persons there assembled, lifting gracefully the flap of his large hat, which was crowned with a black and yellow plume. The captain returned his salute, and both looked at each other for some time without speaking.

"Captain," said the young stranger at last, "I am a Protestant gentleman, and rejoice to meet some of my brethren in religion. If you please, we will sup together."

The captain, favourably impressed already by the distinguished mien and elegant dress of the stranger, answered that he was much honoured. And forthwith Mademoiselle Mila, the gipsy girl of whom we have spoken, made room for the stranger on the bench beside her; and being of a very obliging disposition, gave him her own glass, which the captain promptly filled.

"My name is Dietrich Hornstein," said he, as he clinked glasses with the young man. "You have doubtless heard of Captain Dietrich Hornstein. 'Twas I led the forlorn hope at the battle of Dreux, and at Arnay-le-Duc afterwards."

The stranger understood this indirect way of asking him his own name, and answered, "I am sorry, captain, that I cannot give you a name as famous as your own—as famous, that is to say, on my own account, for my father's has made noise enough in our civil wars. Men call me Bernard de Mergy."

"You tell the name to the right ears," cried the captain, filling his glass to the brim. "I knew your father, M. Bernard de Mergy. I have known him since the first civil war as one knows an intimate friend. His health, Master Bernard."

The captain held out his glass and said a few words in German to the troopers, who at the moment the wine touched his lips threw their hats in the air with a shout.

The host, who took this for a signal of massacre, fell on his knees; and Bernard himself was a little surprised at the exceptional honour. But he thought it his duty not to be behind this German politeness, and gave the captain's health. The bottles, already stoutly attacked before his arrival, could not hold out at this fresh toast.

" Get up, hypocrite," said the captain, turning to the still kneeling host; "get up, and fetch us wine. See you not that the bottles are empty?" And the cornet, to prove the fact, threw one of them at the head of the host, who ran to the cellar.

" 'Tis an insolent rascal," said Mergy: "but you might have done him more harm than you meant if that bottle had gone straight."

" Bah!" said the cornet with a loud laugh; and Mila added, " A Papist's head, though it be emptier than that bottle, is also harder:" whereat the cornet laughed yet louder, and was imitated by all the company, even by Mergy, whose smile, however, was rather for the gipsy's pretty mouth than for her cruel jest. They brought the wine, the supper followed, and after a moment's silence the captain began again with his mouth full:

" I should think I did know M. de Mergy. He was colonel of infantry when the prince made his first attempt. We had the same quarters for two months running at the first siege of Orleans. And how is he now?"

" Well enough, thank God, seeing his great age. He has talked to me often enough of the Reiters and the gallant charges they made at Dreux."

" I knew his elder son, too, your brother, Captain George. I mean before——"

Mergy seemed embarrassed, but the captain went on—

" He was as brave as steel, but hotheaded enough, plague on it! I am sorry for your father; the apostasy must have grieved him much."

Mergy blushed up to his eyes, and stammered some words of excuse for his brother; but it was clear that he judged him even more severely than the captain of Reiters.

" Ah, I see you are vexed," said the captain; " let us drop the subject. He was a loss for the religion and a gain for the King, who they say pays him much honour."

" You come from Paris," said Mergy, seeking to change the conversation; " has the Admiral arrived? You have doubtless seen him. How goes it with him?"

" He was just arriving with the Court from Blois as we left. He is wonderfully well, fresh, and lively; and is good for twenty civil wars yet, honest man. His Majesty pays him so much attention that the Papists are bursting with envy."

" Really? But the King can never do him honour equal to his merit."

" Look you. I saw the King yesterday on the Louvre staircase clasping the Admiral's hand. M. de Guise, who came behind, looked like a whipped hound. And what do you think I thought? It looked to me like the man who shows off the lion at a fair. He makes him give paw like a dog; but though Jack Lion-tamer keeps a brave face on it, he never forgets the claws of the paw he holds. Yes, by my beard, a man might say the King felt the Admiral's claws."

" The Admiral has a long arm," said the cornet, repeating a catchword of the Protestant army.

" He is a handsome man for his years," observed Mademoiselle Mila.

" I would rather have him for lover than a young Papist," retorted Mademoiselle Trudchen, the cornet's friend.

" He is a pillar of the faith," quoth Mergy, not wishing to be behindhand in praise.

" Yes, but he is devilishly strict on the point of discipline," said the captain with a shake of the head. The cornet winked meaningly, and his fat face crumpled itself up in a grimace which he meant for a smile.

" I did not expect," said Mergy, " to hear an old soldier like you, captain, blame the Admiral for keeping strict discipline in his army."

" Oh, yes, of course we must have discipline ; but still soldiers ought to have credit for all the sufferings they go through, and not be forbidden to enjoy themselves when fortune gives them the chance. But bah ! every man has his faults, and though he did hang me, let us drink the Admiral's health."

" The Admiral hanged you !" cried Mergy. " You seem to be in very good case for a hanged man "

" Yes, *sacrament !* He hanged me, but I bear no malice, so here's to him."

Before Mergy could repeat his question the captain filled all the glasses, took off his hat, and made his troopers give a " Hip ! hip ! hurrah !" The glasses empty and the noise quieted, Mergy began again :

" Why did they hang you, captain ?"

" For a mere trifle ; a miserable convent in Saintonge that was sacked, and then burnt by accident."

" But the monks had not all got out of it," interrupted the cornet, roaring with laughter at his own wit.

" Well, what does it matter whether such rascals burn a little sooner or a little later ? Yet the Admiral, would you believe it, M. de Mergy, but the Admiral got seriously angry, had me arrested, and the provost-marshal marked me for his own in the most unceremonious manner. Then all the gentlemen and noblemen of his following, even M. de Lanoue, who, as all men know, has no bowels for the poor soldier ('the knot [*la noue*] ties and does not untie,' as they say), all the captains, in short, begged for my pardon, but he gave them a flat refusal. *Ventre de loup!* what a rage he was in! He chewed his toothpick with fury; and you know the proverb, 'God keep us from M. de Montmorency's prayers and the Admiral's toothpick.' 'God pardon me,' quoth he, 'we must kill Madam Plunder when she is a little girl; if we let her grow a great lady she will kill us.' So there comes me the minister, book under arm, and they take the pair of us beneath a certain oak tree. I can see it now, with a branch sticking out that seemed to have grown on purpose. They put the cord round my neck—and when I think of that cord my throat grows dry as tinder."

"Wet it then," quoth Mila, and she filled him a bumper. He drained it at a gulp, and went on:

"I set my life just at an acorn's fee, and no more, when it occurred to me to say to the Admiral, 'Eh, Monseigneur, is this the way you hang a man who led the forlorn hope at Dreux?' He spat out his toothpick and took another, which I said to myself was a good sign. Then he called Captain Cormier, and whispered in his ear: then he said to the provost, 'Come, up with the fellow!' and turned on his heel. They ran me up, sure enough; but Cormier, like a good fellow, drew sword and slashed the rope, so that I fell from my branch as red as a boiled crayfish."

"I congratulate you," said Mergy, "on having escaped so cheaply." But he looked at the captain curiously, and seemed a little disturbed at finding himself in company with a man who had earned the gallows. In these unlucky times, however, crime was so common that it was impossible to judge it as one would do nowadays. Party atrocities justified reprisal, and religious hatred almost smothered all national sentiment. Besides, to tell the truth, the secret provocations of Mademoiselle Mila, whom he began to think very pretty indeed, and the fumes of the wine, which had more power over his young head than over the seasoned brains of the Reiters, joined in making him feel unusually indulgent towards his companions.

"I kept the captain hidden in a tilted cart for a week," said Mila, "and only let him out at night-time."

"And I," said Trudchen, "I brought him food and drink. He is there to say so."

"The Admiral pretended to be very wroth with Cormier, but all that was only a game arranged between them. As for me, I followed the army long, not daring to show myself to him, till, at the siege of Longnac, he spied me in the trenches, and said, 'Dietrich, my friend, as you have not been hanged, go and get shot,' and he pointed to the breach. I knew what he meant well enough, went stoutly to the assault, and met him next day in the street with my hat in my hand and a bullet-hole through my hat. 'Monseigneur,' said I, 'shooting has the same effect on me as hanging.' So he smiled and gave me his purse, saying, 'There is a new hat for you.' Since which time we have always been good friends. Ah, what a sack that was at the said town of Longnac! My mouth waters at the mere thought of it."

"Such silk dresses!" cried Mila.

"Such plenty of lovely linen!" cried Trudchen.

"What a time we had with the nuns of the great

convent!" said the cornet. "Two hundred horse-arque-
busiers quartered on a hundred nuns!"

"More than twenty of them abjured Popery," said Mila,
"they found the Huguenots so much to their taste."

"'Twas there, too," cried the captain, "that 'twas pretty
to see our *argoulets*[1] watering their horses with priests'
chasubles on their backs, our horses eating their oats off the
altar, and ourselves drinking the priests' good wine in their
silver chalices!"

He turned his head to call for drink, and caught the host
clasping his hands and lifting his eyes to heaven with an
expression of unspeakable horror.

"Idiot!" said the gallant Dietrich Hornstein, shrugging
his shoulders; "how can a man be such a fool as to believe
all the nonsense that Popish priests talk? Why, M. de
Mergy, at Montcontour I killed one of the Duke of Anjou's
gentlemen with a pistol-shot, and when I pulled off his
doublet, what do you think I found on his breast? —a
great piece of silk embroidered all over with saints'
names; he thought it would keep off the balls. By Jove!
I taught him that a Protestant bullet will go through any
scapulary."

"Yes, through scapularies," said the cornet; "but in my
country they sell parchments which really keep you from
shot and sword."

"I would rather have a good steel cuirass, well hammered,
like those that Jacob Leschot makes in the Netherlands,"
said Mergy.

"Ah, but listen," continued the captain; "no doubt it is
possible to be made ball-proof. I myself saw at Dreux a

---

[1] Pioneers, light troops.

gentleman hit by an arquebuss ball right in the centre of the chest; he knew the receipt of ball-proof ointment, and had rubbed himself under his buff coat with it; well, there was not even the red and black mark of a bruise to be seen on him."

"And do not you think that the buff coat you speak of was enough to turn the shot by itself?"

"Ah, you believe in nothing, you Frenchmen. But what would you say if you had seen, as I have, a Silesian gendarme put his hand on the table and the whole company try in vain to make a wound in it with the full force of their daggers? You laugh. You think it impossible. Ask Mila, then. You see that young woman? She comes from a country where wizards are as common as monks here. She is the girl to tell you horrible stories of them. Sometimes in the long autumn evenings, round the camp-fire in the open air, she makes my hair stand on end with her legends."

" I should be charmed to hear one," said Mergy. " Do me that pleasure, fair Mila."

" Yes, Mila," added the captain, " tell us a story while we finish these bottles."

" Listen then," said Mila : " and you, young sir, who believe in nothing, will be good enough, if you please, to keep your doubts to yourself."

" How can you say that I believe in nothing ? " said Mergy in a low voice ; " faith, I believe you have bewitched me already, for I am head-over-ears in love with you."

Mila pushed him gently back, for his lips nearly touched her cheek ; and after glancing slyly right and left to see that all were listening, she thus began :

" Captain, of course you have been at Hamelin ? "

" Never."

" Nor you, cornet ? "

" Nor I."

" What ! can I find no one who has been at Hamelin ? "

" I spent a year there," said a trooper, coming forward.

" Well, Fritz, you saw the church ? "

" Hundreds of times."

" And its stained-glass windows ? "

" Certainly."

" And what did you see painted there ? "

" On the windows ? To the left, I think, there is a tall black man who plays the flute, and little children running after him."

" Just so. Well, I am going to tell you the story of that black man and those children.

" Many years ago the people of Hamelin were tormented by an innumerable multitude of rats, who came from the north in swarms so thick that the earth was black with them, and that a carter would not have dared to drive his horses across a road where the beasts were passing. Everything was devoured in a moment; and it took less time for the rats to eat a barrel of corn in a barn than it takes me to drink a glass of this good wine."

She drank, wiped her mouth, and went on.

" Mouse-traps, rat-traps, snares, poison, all were useless. They brought a boat-load of eleven hundred cats from Bremen, but it did no good at all. For each thousand rats killed ten thousand appeared, hungrier than the first. In short, if the plague had not been stayed, not a grain of corn would have remained in Hamelin town, and all the dwellers therein must have died of hunger.

" Now on a certain Friday there came before the burgomaster a tall man, swarthy and parched of aspect, with large eyes, and a mouth from ear to ear. He was dressed in a red jerkin, a pointed hat, wide breeches trimmed with ribbons, grey stockings, and shoes with flame-coloured rosettes. He had a little leather wallet slung at his side. I think I see him now."

All eyes turned involuntarily to the wall at which Mila was staring.

" *You* saw him then?" asked Mergy.

" No, not I, 'twas my grandmother, and she remembered him so well that she could have drawn his portrait."

" And what said he to the burgomaster?"

" He offered, for a fee of a hundred ducats, to deliver the city from its scourge; and, as you may think, the burgomaster and the citizens said 'Done' at once. Forthwith the stranger drew from his wallet a flute of bronze, and taking up his station in the market-place in front of the church (but with his back to it, mind), he began to play an air so strange that

no German flute-player has ever played the like. And as
they heard this air, there flocked around him from garret
and rat-hole, from rafter and tile, rats and mice by hundreds
and thousands. And the stranger, piping still, bent his way
to the river Weser, and there, stripping off his hose, he went
into the water followed by all the rats of Hamelin, who were
drowned straightway. But one remained in all the city, and
you shall hear wherefore. The magician (for such he was)
asked a laggard rat who had not yet got into the water why
Klaus, the white rat, had not come. 'My lord,' said the
rat, 'he is so old that he cannot walk.' 'Go and fetch him
yourself,' said the magician; and the rat turned tail, and
went to the town, whence he came back quickly with a great
old, old, white rat, so old that he could not drag himself
along; and the two rats, the young one dragging the old
by the tail, both plunged in the Weser, and were drowned
like their fellows. And so the town was cleared. But when
the stranger appeared at the town-hall to draw the promised
recompense, the burgomaster and the citizens, remembering
that they had nothing more to fear from the rats, and thinking that they could make short work of a friendless man, were
not ashamed to offer him ten ducats instead of the hundred
that they had promised. The stranger protested; they gave
him a flat refusal. He threatened them that he would
exact a far higher price if they did not carry out their
bargain. The citizens burst out laughing at the threat, and
showed him the door, calling him a 'fine rat-catcher,' which
insult the children of the town repeated as they followed
him up the streets to the New Gate. Next Friday at noon-
day the stranger reappeared on the market-place, but this
time with a purple hat, cocked in a singular fashion. He
drew from his wallet a flute quite different from the other,

and as soon as he had begun to play all the boys of the city from six years old to fifteen followed him out of the town precincts."

"And did the men of Hamelin let them be carried off quietly?" asked Mergy and the captain together.

"They followed them to Koppenberg Hill, close to a cavern which is now stopped up. The flute-player entered the cave and all the children with him. For a time they heard the sound of the flute; little by little it died away; then they heard nothing. The children had vanished, and never afterwards was aught heard of them."

The gipsy stopped to watch the effect of her story on the countenances of her hearers; but the Reiter who had been at Hamelin took up her words and said, "The story is so true, that when they speak at Hamelin of anything out of the way, they say, 'That happened ten or twenty years after our children departed;' for instance, 'The lord of Falkenstein sacked the town sixty years after our children departed.'"

"But the strangest thing of all," said Mila, "is that at the very same time there appeared, far off in Transylvania, certain children who spoke good German, and who could not tell from whence they came. They married in the country, and taught their tongue to their own offspring, whence it comes that, at this day, men speak German in Transylvania."

"And those were the Hamelin children, transported thither by the devil?" said Mergy, smiling.

"By heaven 'tis true," said the captain, "for I have been in Transylvania myself, and I know that they talk German while all round men jabber an infernal jargon." And, indeed, there is plenty of evidence produced every day which is not a whit better than the captain's.

"Shall I tell you your fortune?" said Mila to Mergy.

"By all means," said he, putting his left arm round the gipsy's waist, while he held out his right palm.

Mila looked at it for nearly five minutes without speaking, but shaking her head now and then with a thoughtful air.

"Well, pretty child, shall I win the woman I love?"

Mila tapped his hand. "Here is luck and ill luck," quoth she; "blue eyes bring harm and good. The worst of it is, you will shed your own blood."

The captain and the cornet both held their tongues, seeming to be equally struck with the sinister ending of the prophecy; and the host crossed himself vigorously in the corner.

"I will believe you are really a witch," said Mergy. "if you can tell me what I am going to do directly?"

"You are going to kiss me," whispered the gipsy in his ear.

"She *is* a witch." cried Mergy, kissing her. And he continued to talk low to the fair fortune-teller, while they seemed to get on better and better together each moment.

Trudchen took up a kind of mandolin, reasonably well provided with strings, and played a German march as overture. Then when a ring of soldiers had gathered round her

she sang in her own tongue a war song which the Reiters
chorussed at the top of their voices. But the captain, not
to be outdone, began to sing too, at a pitch loud enough to
break the glasses, an old Huguenot song, of which the tune
was as barbarous as the words :

> " Condé he is dead,
> But the Admiral's at our head,
> And La Rochefoucauld so stout,
> To drive the Papists out—
>   Out, out, out." [1]

Whereat all the Reiters, heated with wine, began to sing
each a different air. The dishes and the bottles covered
the floor in fragments ; the kitchen echoed with oaths,
shouts of laughter, and drinking songs. But soon sleep,
helped by the Orleans wine, made his power felt by
most of the actors in this scene of riot. The soldiers
stretched themselves on the benches ; the cornet, after
posting two sentinels at the door, staggered to bed ; the
captain, who still preserved a respect for straight lines,
climbed, without a lurch, the staircase leading to the host's
chamber, which he had chosen as the best in the inn.

But what had become of Mergy and the gipsy ? Before
the captain began to sing they had disappeared together.

[1] [Literally, " The Prince of Condé, He has been killed ; But M. l'Amiral
Is still on horseback, With La Rochefoucauld, To hunt all the papists,
Papists, papists, papists ! "]—*Translator's note.*

CHAPTER II.

THE MORROW OF A REVEL.

"Chairman, I say I will have my money instantly."
MOLIÈRE, *Les Précieuses Ridicules.*

DAY had long dawned when Mergy woke, his head still something flustered with the memories of the night before. His clothes lay scattered about the chamber, and his portmanteau was open on the floor. Sitting up in bed, he gazed for some time at this scene of confusion, rubbing his head as if to get his ideas into order. His countenance expressed at once weariness, astonishment, and anxiety.

Meanwhile, a heavy step was heard on the stone stair

F

that led to the room. The door was opened without the formality of a knock, and the host entered with an air even sulkier than that of yesterday; but now his looks plainly showed a touch of insolence which had taken the place of fear. He glanced round the room, and crossed himself as if horrified at such disorder.

"Ah! my young sir," he said, "still abed? Come, get up, for there are accounts to settle between us."

Mergy, with an appalling yawn, put one leg out of bed. "What is all this muddle? Why is my portmanteau open?" he asked in a tone at least as ill-tempered as the host's.

"Why? Why?" answered he. "How do I know? What do I care for your portmanteau? You have put my house in far worse plight. But by my blessed patron Saint Eustace you shall pay me for it."

As he spoke, Mergy drew on his scarlet breeches, and in the motion his pocket gaped, and his purse fell out. The sound must have been different from that which he expected, for he picked it up at once anxiously and opened it.

"I have been robbed!" he cried, turning to the host. For instead of twenty gold crowns which his purse had held, there were but two. But Master Eustace shrugged his shoulders and smiled contemptuously.

"I have been robbed!" repeated Mergy, hastily buckling his belt. "I had twenty gold crowns in this purse, and I insist on having them back. 'Twas in your house they were taken from me."

"By my beard I am glad of it," cried the host insolently; "that will teach you to foregather with witches and thieves. But," added he in a lower tone, "like draws to like. All these gallow-birds of a feather—heretics, sorcerers, and thieves—flock together."

" What do you say, scoundrel ? " cried Mergy, all the more angry that he felt the justice of the reproach, and, as a man usually does when he is in the wrong, caught eagerly at a cause of quarrel.

" I say," said the host, with arms akimbo and uplifted voice,—" I say that you have broken everything in my house, and I insist that you shall pay me to the last penny."

" I will pay my score, and not a farthing over. Where is Captain Corn—Captain Hornstein ? "

" Two hundred bottles," cried Master Eustace, still rais ing his voice,—" two hundred bottles of my good old wine have been drunk. But you are answerable for them."

Mergy was now completely dressed.

" Where is the captain ? " he cried in a voice of thunder.

" He has been gone more than two hours ; and may he go to the devil with all the other Huguenots—till we can find time to burn them."

A sound box on the ear was the only answer that occurred to Mergy ; and the suddenness and force of the blow made the host fall back two steps. His grasp sought the horn handle of a great knife which protruded from his breeches pocket, and had he yielded to this first motion of wrath, some serious mischief would no doubt have happened. But prudence arrested anger, and made him notice that Mergy was stretching out his own hand to the bed-head where hung a long rapier. So he gave up the unequal contest, and hurried downstairs yelling " Murder ! Fire ! "

In possession of the field of battle, but exceedingly anxious as to what would come after the victory, Mergy finished buckling on his belt, stuck his pistols therein, shut his portmanteau, and, holding it in his hand, resolved to lodge his complaint with the nearest magistrate. He

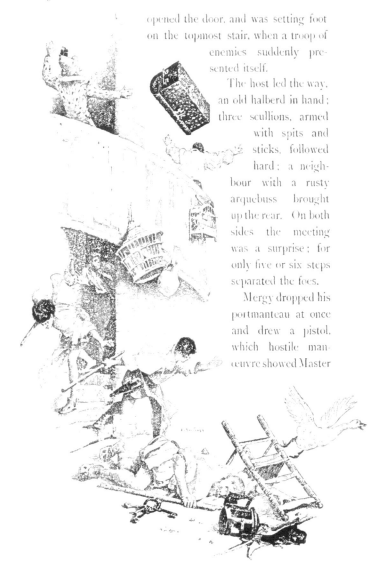

opened the door, and was setting foot
on the topmost stair, when a troop of
enemies suddenly pre-
sented itself.

The host led the way,
an old halberd in hand;
three scullions, armed
with spits and
sticks, followed
hard; a neigh-
bour with a rusty
arquebuss brought
up the rear. On both
sides the meeting
was a surprise; for
only five or six steps
separated the foes.

Mergy dropped his
portmanteau at once
and drew a pistol,
which hostile man-
œuvre showed Master

Eustace and his suite how faulty their order of battle was.
Like the Persians at the battle of Salamis, they had forgotten to take up a position where their numbers could
deploy with advantage. The only one of them who carried
firearms could not use them without endangering his companions in front, while the Huguenot's pistols, enfilading
the staircase, seemed likely to knock them all over. They
heard the click of the pistol as Mergy cocked it, and an
actual detonation could not have frightened them more.
With one accord the hostile column turned tail and fled, to
seek in the kitchen a roomier and more advantageous battle-
field. In the disorder which inevitably accompanies a hurried retreat, the host, wishing to shift his halberd, entangled
it in his legs and fell. Like a generous foe, disdaining to
make use of his actual weapons, Mergy contented himself
with hurling his portmanteau at the enemy, and this, falling
like a mass of rock, and moving faster as it fell from stair
to stair, finished the rout. The staircase remained clear of
foes, with the broken halberd as a trophy.

Mergy at once made for the kitchen, where the foe had
re-formed in a single line. The arquebusier had his weapon
in position, and was blowing his lighted match. The host,
covered with blood (for his nose had been badly bruised in
the fall), remained behind his friends, like the wounded
Menelaus behind the Grecian ranks; while, in default of
Machaon or Podalirius, his wife, with dishevelled hair and
coif unbound, staunched his face with a dirty napkin. There
was no hesitation in Mergy's conduct. He walked straight
up to the man with the arquebuss and held the muzzle of a
pistol to his breast.

"Drop your match, or you die!" he said.

The match fell to earth, and Mergy, setting his foot on

the lighted end, extinguished it; whereupon all the allies at once threw down their arms.

"As for you," said Mergy to the innkeeper, "the small lesson I have given you will no doubt teach you to treat strangers more politely. If I chose I could have your licence withdrawn by the bailiff here; but I bear no malice. Come, what do I owe you for my own score?"

Master Eustace, observing that he had uncocked the terrible pistol, and was as he spoke slipping it back into his belt, plucked up a little courage, and while continuing to staunch his wounds, muttered in a melancholy manner:

"You break the dishes, you beat people, you break good Christian noses, you make hell's own riot. After that, I do not see how you can make it up to an honest man."

"Come," went on Mergy smiling, "I will pay you for your nose at my valuation of it. As for your broken crockery, you must go to the Reiters for that; it is their business. And now what do I owe you for my supper yesterday?"

The host looked at his wife, his scullions, and his neighbour, as if to ask at once their counsel and their help.

"The Reiters! the Reiters!" said he. "A man does not easily see the colour of *their* money. The captain gave me three livres and the cornet a kick."

Mergy took out one of the two gold crowns which he had left. "Come," said he, "we will part good friends." And he threw it to Master Eustace, who, instead of catching it, scornfully let it fall on the floor.

"A crown!" he cried. "A crown for a hundred broken bottles! A crown for sacking a house and beating its people!"

"A crown—only a crown!" chimed in his wife in an

equally mournful tone. "Catholic gentlemen come here sometimes and make a disturbance, but at least they know the value of things."

Had Mergy been more in funds he would no doubt have kept up his party's reputation for free-handedness. As it was, he replied drily, "Very like; but these Catholic gentlemen have not been robbed. Make up your minds," he added ; "take the crown or you will have nothing," and he made a step forward as if to pick it up. The hostess seized it instantly. "Come, bring me my horse ; and you, fellow, drop that spit and carry my portmanteau."

"Your horse, sir?" said one of Master Eustace's men, making a face. But the host himself lifted his head in spite of his vexation, and his eyes sparkled with spiteful pleasure.

"Oh, yes! I will bring him myself, my good lord ; I will bring you your good horse." And he went out with the napkin still pressed to his face, while Mergy followed.

You may guess his surprise when he saw in the place of the bonny chestnut steed which had carried him thither a little old broken-kneed piebald, whose appearance was still further improved by a great scar on the head ; while instead of his saddle of fine Flanders velvet he beheld a leathern troop-saddle mounted with iron.

"What do you mean by that?" he cried. "Where is my horse?"

"Your lordship must go and ask the Protestant Reiter gentlemen that," said the host with feigned humility. "The worthy strangers carried him off with them, no doubt mistaking the two, as they were so like one another."

"'Tis a fine horse," said a scullion ; "I would bet he is not more than a twenty-year-old."

" No one can say he is no charger," quoth another ; " look at the sword-wound on his forehead."

" His coat stares finely," said a third ; " 'tis like a minister's, black and white."

Mergy went into the stable, which was quite empty.

" And why did you let them take my horse ?" he cried in a fury.

" By'r Lady, fair sir," said the stableman, " the trumpeter took him away, and told me that you had arranged to exchange him."

Mergy, choking with rage, and not knowing what to be at in this accumulation of misfortunes, muttered between his teeth, " I will find the captain, and he shall do me justice on this rascal thief."

To which the host replied, " Your lordship will do well ; for this Captain what's-his-name looked like a very honest fellow." (Now Mergy had himself been thinking that the captain, if he had not ordered the theft, must have winked at it.) " And," added the host, "you can get back your gold crowns from the young lady at the same time. She must have made a mistake, no doubt, in packing up her things by owl's light."

" Shall I fasten your lordship's portmanteau on your lordship's horse ?" said the ostler, with the most intolerable air of mock respect.

Mergy understood that the longer he stayed the more of these rascals' jests he should have to endure, so as soon as the portmanteau was fastened on, he jumped into his awkward saddle ; but the horse, feeling that he had a new master, conceived a malicious desire to find out whether his new master could ride. He was not long, however, in discovering that he had to do with a skilful horseman, in

less temper than usual to stand any nonsense, and so, after
lashing out a little, and being well rewarded by the digging
in of some exceedingly sharp spurs, he wisely made up his
mind to submit, and broke into a steady trot. But he had
used up some of his strength in the fight with his rider;
and, as usually happens to jades in such a case, he fell,
stumbling, as they say, with all four feet at once. Our
hero picked himself up quickly, a little bruised, but much
more angry at the jeers which were raised behind him. He
even hesitated for a moment whether he should go and take
vengeance with the flat of his sword; but on reflection he
contented himself with making as though he had not heard
the distant insults, and took at a slower pace the Orleans
road, pursued for a time by troops of children, the elders
singing the ballad of " Jehan Petaquin,"[1] while the little ones
cried at the top of their voices, " Faggots! faggots for the
Huguenot!"

After riding in sufficiently bad spirits for half a league or
so he reflected that he would not be likely to catch up the
Reiters that day; that his horse was probably by this time
sold; that at any rate it was scarcely doubtful that these
gentry would not give him up. Little by little Mergy
made up his mind to the loss; and as in the case of his
horse being gone for good he had nothing to do on the
way to Orleans, he made once more for Paris, taking a
cross road so as to avoid passing the unlucky inn which
had witnessed his disasters. Little by little, having accustomed himself early to look upon the bright side of things,
he came to the conclusion that he was on the whole fortunate in getting off so cheaply, for he might have been
completely stripped, not to say murdered, while as it was

---

[1] An absurd personage in an old folk-song.

G

he had a gold crown in his pocket, almost all his clothes
intact, and a horse who, ugly as he was, could carry him.
Also, to tell the truth, the memory of the fair Mila made
him more than once smile.   Indeed, after a few hours' ride
and a good breakfast, he felt positively affected by the
girl's scrupulous delicacy in taking only eighteen pieces
from a purse that held twenty.   It was harder to stomach
the loss of his good chestnut; but he was bound to admit that
a thief more hardened than the trumpeter would have taken
his horse without leaving him another.   And so he reached
Paris that evening, just before the gates shut, and took up
his abode at an inn in the Rue Saint Jacques.

CHAPTER III.

THE YOUNG COURTIERS.

Iachimo. The ring is won.
Posthumus. The stone's too hard to come by.
Iachimo. Not a whit, your lady being so easy."
SHAKESPEARE, *Cymbeline.*

MERGY'S object in coming to Paris was to obtain strong recommendations to the Admiral Coligny, and a commission in the army which was about, men said, to fight in Flanders under that great captain's orders. He hoped that certain friends of his father's, to whom he brought

letters, would support his demands and would introduce
him to the King's Court as well as to the Admiral, who had
a kind of court of his own.   He knew that his brother was
high in favour ; but he was as yet quite undecided whether
to seek an interview with him or not.   George de Mergy's
apostasy had almost entirely cut him off from his relations,
who regarded him as a stranger—a family split which
religious differences made by no means uncommon at
the time.   For a great while George's father had forbidden
the apostate's name to be uttered in his hearing, and had
justified his severity by the text, " If thy right eye offend
thee, pluck it out."   And although young Bernard was by
no means of the same inflexible temper, his brother's change
of opinions appeared to him a stain on the family honour,
and his fraternal affection had naturally suffered in consequence.

But before deciding on the course which he should take
as regarded his brother, and even before presenting his
letters of recommendation, he thought he had better see to
the filling of his empty purse, and with this object set out
from his inn to visit a goldsmith on the Pont St. Michel,
who owed the family moneys which he was empowered to
claim.

At the bridge-foot he met some elegantly dressed young
men, who, walking arm-in-arm, almost entirely obstructed
the narrow passage left on the bridge by the throng of
shops and booths, which rose like two parallel walls, and
completely hid the view of the river from the passers-by.
Behind these gentlemen came their lackeys, each holding
sheathed in his hands one of the long double-edged swords
called " duellers," and a dagger with so large a shell that it
could be used at need for a shield.   Perhaps the weight of

these weapons was too much for the young gentlemen, or else they were pleased to show the world that they had richly-dressed serving-men. They seemed in good humour, to judge by their continual shouts of laughter. If a well-dressed woman passed by, they saluted her with a mixture of politeness and impertinence, while several of the mad-caps amused themselves by rudely elbowing certain grave citizens in black cloaks, who went off grumbling a thousand curses on the insolence of the courtiers. One only of the group walked with bowed head, and seemed to take no share whatever in their amusements.

" Why, d ——e, George ! " cried another, clapping him on the shoulder, " you are getting desperately sulky. It is a full quarter of an hour since you have opened your mouth. Are you thinking of turning Carthusian ? "

The name " George " made Mergy start ; but he did not hear what the person so addressed answered.

" I will bet a hundred pistoles," went on the first speaker, " that he is still in love with some paragon of virtue. I am sorry for you, my poor friend ; it is certainly bad luck to find any mistress unkind in Paris."

" Go to Rudbeck the wizard," said another; " he will give you a potion to make her love you."

" Perhaps," said a third, " our friend the captain is in love with a nun. These devils of Huguenots, converted or unconverted, always mean mischief to the spouses of Christ."

A voice, which Mergy knew at once, replied sadly—

" Faith ! I should not be as miserable as I am, if nothing but love-matters were at stake. But," he added, dropping his voice, " De Pons, to whom I gave a letter for my father, has returned and tells me that he insists on having nothing to do with me."

" Your father is a chip of the old block," said one of the young men. " He was one of the Huguenots who tried Amboise."

At that moment Captain George, who had turned his head, perceived Mergy, and with a cry of surprise and open arms he sprang towards him. Mergy lost not a moment in holding out his own hands, and hugged him to his breast. It may be that had the meeting been less sudden, he might have tried to steel himself up ; but the surprise gave nature her rights. From that moment they looked on each other as friends who meet after a long journey.

After the first embrace and the first inquiries, Captain George turned to his friends, some of whom had stood still to contemplate the proceeding.

" Sirs," said he, " you have been witness to this unexpected meeting. Forgive me if I leave you to entertain a brother whom I have not seen for more than seven years."

" But we do not mean you to leave us at all to-day. Dinner is ordered, and you must come." And he who spoke seized George at the same time by his cloak.

" Béville is right," said another ; " we will not let you go."

" Why, *mordieu !* " said Béville, " let your brother dine with us. Instead of one good fellow, we shall have two."

" Pardon me," thereupon said Mergy, " but I have much business to do to-day ; I have letters to deliver—— "

" You can deliver them to-morrow."

" They must be delivered to-day. And," added Mergy, smiling a little shamefacedly, " I must tell you that I am penniless, and I must really go and look for some money—— "

" A pretty excuse, good faith ! " cried they all. " We cannot possibly let you refuse to dine with good Christians like us that you may go and borrow from Jews ! "

"Come, my good friend," said Béville, ostentatiously shaking a long silk purse which swung at his girdle, "look upon me as your banker. The dice have dealt kindly with me for a whole fortnight."

"Come along; let us not waste time, but go and dine at the Black Boy," said all the young men.

Captain George looked at his brother, who was still uncertain. "After all, you will have plenty of time to deliver your letters. As for money, I have some; so come with us. You will see how we live in Paris."

Mergy allowed himself to be persuaded, and his brother introduced him formally to all his friends in turn: the Baron de Vaudreuil, the Chevalier de Rheiney, the Vicomte de Béville, and so on. They were prodigal of caresses to the newcomer, who was obliged to embrace them all one after the other. Béville was the last to exchange salutes with him.

"Oh! oh!" quoth he. "Curse me, comrade, but I smell a heretic. My gold chain to a pistole that you are of the religion."

"'Tis true, sir; though I am not as good a member of it as I ought to be."

"There! can I not tell a Huguenot among a thousand? *Ventre de loup!* how serious our Methodists look when they talk of their religion."

"I think one should never speak jestingly on such a subject."

"M. de Mergy is right," said Vaudreuil; "and as for you, Béville, this ill-timed pleasantry of yours on sacred things will bring you ill luck."

"There is a saint for you!" said Béville to Mergy. "He is the most outrageous libertine of us all; and yet he gives us a sermon now and then."

"Do not make me out worse than I am, Béville," said Vaudreuil. "If I am a libertine it is because I cannot subdue the flesh; but at least I respect what ought to be respected."

"For my part, I respect my mother; she is the only honest woman I have ever known. For the rest, my good fellow, Catholics, Huguenots, Turks, and Jews are all the same to me; I rate their quarrels at the price of a broken spur-rowel."

"Infidel!" muttered Vaudreuil; and he crossed himself over the mouth, holding his handkerchief to hide it meanwhile as much as he could.

"You must know, Bernard," said Captain George, "that you must not look among us for disputants like your and my learned master, Theobald Wolfsteinius. We do not care much for theological discussions, and, thank heaven, we employ our time better."

"Yet perhaps," said Mergy rather bitterly, "it might have been better for you had you listened attentively to the learned dissertations of the worthy minister you have named."

"A truce to that, little brother; we may talk of it again perchance. I know what you think of me, but never mind. We are not here to talk of such matters. I believe I am a man of honour, and you will find it out some day. Drop the subject; we must think now only of amusement." And he passed his hand over his brow as if to drive off painful thoughts.

Mergy only whispered, "Dear brother!" and pressed his hand. George replied by a similar pressure, and both hurried after their companions, who were somewhat in advance of them.

As they passed in front of the Louvre, whence crowds of

well-dressed people issued, the captain and his friends gave bow or embrace to almost all the noblemen they met, at the same time introducing young Mergy, who in this way made prompt acquaintance with a vast number of celebrated personages of the day. As he did so he was told their nicknames (for everyone of any note had his nickname then), as well as the scandalous stories which were reported about them.

"Do you see," they said, "that counsellor, so pale and so yellow? That is Master Petrus de Finibus, otherwise Pierre Séguier, who makes so much ado, and so cleverly, that in everything he undertakes he always gains his ends. There is Thoré de Montmorency, 'little Captain Burn-the-benches.' There is his grace the Archbishop of Bottles,[1] who is pretty steady on his mule, because he has not dined yet. Here is one of the heroes of your own party, the valiant Count de la Rochefoucauld, surnamed the Cabbage-killer. In the last war he riddled with shot an unlucky plot of cabbages which his bad sight made him take for Lanzknechts."

In less than a quarter of an hour Mergy knew the names of the lovers of almost all the Court ladies, and the number of duels which had been brought about by the beauty of each. He remarked that the more deaths a lady had been the cause of, the higher did her fame rank. Thus Madame de Courtavel, whose recognized lover had killed two of his rivals, was far better reputed than the unlucky Countess de Pomerande, who had but one miserable duel (with a mere scratch as the result) to her name.

A lady of stately figure, mounted on a white mule, which

---

[1] The Archbishop of Guise.

11

was led by an equerry and followed by two lackeys, attracted Mergy's attention. Her dress
was of the new-
est cut, and
stiff with em-
broidery. As
far as he could
judge she must
be beautiful; but
at that time, as
is well known, ladies never went
out of doors save masked. Her
mask was of black velvet, and

you could see, or rather guess from what showed through the eye-holes, that she had skin of a dazzling whiteness and eyes of a dark blue. She slackened her mule's pace as she passed the young men, and even seemed to look somewhat attentively at Mergy, whose face was strange to her. Plumed hats swept the earth on the path before her; and she bent her head gracefully to return the numerous salutes of a double row of admirers as she passed. As she disappeared a puff of wind lifted the hem of her long satin gown, and showed, as by a flash of lightning, a little slipper of white velvet and some inches of pink silk stocking.

"Who is that lady whom everyone salutes?" asked Mergy with some interest.

"What! in love already?" cried Béville. "Ah, well, it is always her way; Huguenots and Papists alike, all fall in love with Countess Diane de Turgis."

"She is one of the Court beauties," added George; "one of the most dangerous of Circes for our young gallants. Nor is the fortress easy to carry, confound it."

"What is *her* record of duels?" asked Mergy, smiling.

"Oh, she is only in her scores," answered the Baron de Vaudreuil. "But the best of it is that she wanted to fight herself. She sent a regular challenge to another Court lady who had taken precedence of her."

"A pretty story!" cried Mergy.

"She would not have been the first of our time," said George, "if she had actually fought. She sent, really sent, a perfectly regular, correct challenge to Madame de Sainte-Foix, offering a duel to the death with sword and dagger, stripped to the shift, just as a *raffiné*[1] duellist would do."

"I should like to have been one of their seconds to see them both in that costume," said the Chevalier de Rheincy.

"And did the fight come off?" said Mergy.

"No," said George; "the matter was made up."

"That is to say, *he* made it up," said Vaudreuil, "for he was Madame de Sainte-Foix's lover at the time."

"Fie! fie! no more than yourself," quoth George with a very discreet air.

"Madame de Turgis is like Vaudreuil," said Béville, "she hashes up religion and the way of the world together; wants to fight a duel (which is, I believe, mortal sin), and hears two masses a day."

"Do let my mass and me alone!" cried Vaudreuil.

"Yes; she goes to mass," said Rheincy, "but it is to show herself unmasked."

"Why, 'tis just for that that so many women go to mass,"

---

[1] The term of the day for a professional duellist.

remarked Mergy, pleased at finding a chance of jesting at the religion which was not his own.

"And to meeting, too," said Béville. "When the sermon is done, the lights are put out, and then there are fine doings. 'Sdeath! it tempts me terribly to turn Lutheran."

"And you believe those absurd stories?" said Mergy disdainfully.

"Do I believe them? Why, little Ferrand, whom we all know, used to go to meeting at Orleans to see a notary's wife. A very fine woman, by Jove! He used to make my mouth water by talking of her. He could see her nowhere else; and luckily a Huguenot friend of his had given him the password, so he got into the meeting-house; and I leave you to guess whether our comrade employed his time well in the dark or not."

"But that is impossible," said Mergy drily.

"Impossible? Pray why?"

"Because no Protestant would be so base as to let a Papist into meeting."

The answer was greeted with loud laughter.

"What!" said Vaudreuil. "You think that because a man is a Huguenot he can neither be a thief, nor a traitor, nor a pimp?"

"He must have fallen from the moon!" cried Rheiney.

"For my part," said Béville, "if I had to send a billet to a Huguenot beauty, I should go straight to her minister."

"Because, I suppose," answered Mergy, "you are accustomed to employ your priests in the same way."

"Our priests?" said Vaudreuil, reddening angrily.

"I pray you, leave off this tiresome talk," interrupted George, who noticed the offensive sharpness of each repartee. "Let us leave all the canters of all the sects alone.

I vote that the first who says 'Huguenot,' 'Papist,' 'Protestant,' or 'Catholic' shall pay forfeit."

"Agreed!" cried Béville. "He shall pay for a round of the good Cahors wine at the inn where we are going to dine." And there was silence for a moment.

"Since poor Lannoy was killed before Orleans, Madame de Turgis has had no known lover," said George, who wished to divert his friends from theological ideas.

"Who would dare to assert that a lady of Paris has no lover?" cried Béville. "'Tis certain that Comminges presses her hard."

"That is the reason," said Vaudreuil, "that young Navarette gave up; he was afraid of such a redoubtable rival."

"Is Comminges jealous, then?" asked the captain.

"Like a tiger," answered Béville; "and he declares he will kill anyone who dares love the fair countess; so that in order not to be left without any lover at all, she must make up her mind to take Comminges."

"Who is this fire-eater?" asked Mergy, who, without quite knowing why, felt a lively curiosity as to everything concerning the Countess de Turgis.

"He is," answered Rheincy, "one of our most famous *raffinés*; and as you come from the country, I will explain our Court lingo to you. A *raffiné* is an accomplished gentleman—a man who fights when another's cloak touches his own, when a man spits within four feet of him, or, in short, for any other equally reasonable reason."

"Comminges," said Vaudreuil, "took a man one day to the Pré-aux-Clercs;[1] they doffed their coats and drew swords. 'Are you not Berny of Auvergne?' said Com-

---

[1] The *locus classicus* of duels at the time. It lay in front of the Louvre, in the space between the Rue des Petits-Augustins and the Rue du Bac.

minges. ' No,' said the other ; ' my name is Villéquier, and
I come from Normandy.' ' That is a pity,' said Comminges ;
' I have mistaken my man. But as I have challenged you,
we must fight.' And he killed him merrily."

Each one added some instance of Comminges' skill or
his quarrelsome temper ; the subject was fertile, and the
conversation lasted them till they were out of the town, at
the Black Boy. This was an inn placed in a garden near
the site where the Tuileries, begun in 1564, was in process
of building. Many more gentlemen of George's friends
met them there, and they sat down to table a numerous
company.

Mergy, who sat by Vaudreuil's side, noticed that his
neighbour in sitting down crossed himself and muttered
with shut eyes and in a low voice this singular grace :
*Laus Deo, pax vivis, salutem defuncti, et beata viscera vir-
ginis Mariæ quæ portaverunt æterni Patris Filium.*

" Do you know Latin, Baron ? " asked Mergy.

" What ! you heard my grace ? "

" Yes ; but I confess that I did not understand it."

" To tell you the truth, I do not understand Latin myself,
and have no clear idea what the prayer means ; but I learnt
it from one of my aunts, who found it very efficacious, and
since I have used it I have been well satisfied with the
result."

" I think it must be Catholic Latin, and therefore we
Huguenots cannot comprehend it."

" A forfeit ! a forfeit ! " cried Béville and Captain George
at once. Mergy submitted with a good grace ; and fresh
bottles, which promptly put the company in good humour,
were set on the table.

The conversation soon became noisier, and Mergy availed

himself of the tumult to talk to his brother without attending to what was going on round them. But this aside was interrupted at the end of the second course by the noise of a violent dispute between two of the guests.

"'Tis false!" cried the Chevalier de Rheincy.

"False!" said Vaudreuil, his naturally pale face becoming corpse-like in hue.

"She is the most virtuous, the chastest of women!" went on the chevalier.

Vaudreuil smiled bitterly and shrugged his shoulders. All eyes were fixed upon the disputants, and each man, in a sort of silent neutrality, seemed to be waiting for the upshot of the quarrel.

"What is the matter, sirs? and what is this noise for?" asked the captain, ready as usual to prevent a breach of the peace.

"Our friend the chevalier," said Béville placidly, " insists that Madame de Sillery, his mistress, is chaste; while our friend Vaudreuil declares that she is not, and that he has reason to know it."

The laugh which followed increased Rheincy's rage, and he fixed eyes of fury on both Vaudreuil and Béville.

"I could show letters of hers," said Vaudreuil.

"I dare you to do so!" cried the chevalier.

"Well," said Vaudreuil, with a very evil sneer on his face, "I will read one to these gentlemen; they may know her writing as well as myself, for I am not coxcomb enough to boast the monopoly of her letters or her favours either. Here is a note I received this very day," and he made as if he would rummage his pocket for a letter.

"You lie in your throat!"

The table was too broad for the baron's hand to reach

his foe, who sat right opposite him ; but he cried, " I will drive that 'lie' down your own till it chokes you!" And he flung a bottle at his adversary's head as he spoke. Rheincy dodged the blow, and upsetting his chair in his haste, sprang to the wall to take down his sword which hung there.

All rose, some to interpose in the quarrel, most to keep clear of it.

" Stop, you madmen," cried George, getting in front of the baron, who was nearest him ; " ought two friends to fight for the sake of a wench ? "

" A bottle flung at one's head is as bad as a blow," said Béville coolly. " Come, chevalier, my friend, out with your sword."

" Fair play ! fair play ! a ring !" cried almost all the guests.

" Shut the door, Jack," calmly said the host of the Black Boy, who was quite used to scenes of this kind. " If the police were to pass it might interrupt the gentlemen, and do harm to the house."

" Will you fight in a tavern-room like drunken Lanz-knechts ?" persisted George, anxious to gain time. " At least wait till to-morrow."

" To-morrow be it," said Rheincy, offering to sheath his sword.

" Our little chevalier is afraid," said Vaudreuil ; whereat Rheincy, thrusting aside those in his way, dashed on his enemy. Both attacked furiously, but Vaudreuil had had time to twist a napkin carefully round his left arm, and he used this with skill to ward off cuts, while Rheincy, who had neglected a similar precaution, was wounded in the left hand at the first passes. But he fought on bravely, shouting to his foot-boy to bring him his poniard. Béville stopped the

I

lackey, declaring that as Vaudreuil had no dagger his foe
must have none.   Some of the chevalier's friends protested,
sharp words were exchanged, and the duel might have turned
into a general affray if Vaudreuil had not ended it by striking his enemy down with a severe wound in the breast.
He set his foot on
Rheiney's sword to

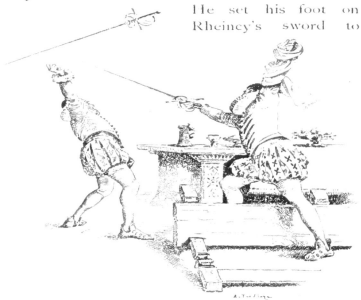

prevent his picking it up, and raised his
own to give the *coup de grâce* :—a piece of
savagery which the duelling rules of the
time permitted.

"Kill a disarmed foe?" cried George; and he
wrested Vaudreuil's sword from his hand.

The chevalier's wound was not mortal, but he bled freely.
They bandaged him up as best they could with napkins,

while he muttered with a forced laugh that the matter was not at an end. Soon there appeared a monk and a surgeon, who wrangled for some time as to which should take charge of the wounded man. The surgeon got the better, and having made them carry his patient to the Seine-bank, he conveyed him in a boat to his lodgings. Meanwhile some of the servants took away the bloody napkins and washed the floor, while others set fresh bottles on the table. As for Vaudreuil, after very carefully wiping his sword, he sheathed it, crossed himself, and with unruffled calm drew a letter from his pocket, requested silence, and read the first line, which excited roars of laughter—

"My darling, that troublesome chevalier who pesters me——"

"Let us go," said Mergy to his brother, with an expression of disgust. The captain followed him, and the general attention paid to the letter prevented their departure from being noticed.

CHAPTER IV.

THE CONVERT.

"Don Juan. What? You take what I have just said for current coin ; and you believe that my mouth speaks in unison with my heart ?"

MOLIÈRE, *Le Festin de Pierre.*

THE captain returned to town with his brother, and took him to his lodgings. They spoke little as they walked thither ; for the scene which they had just witnessed had left on them a painful impression, which made them silent in spite of themselves. Yet the quarrel, and the irregular duel which followed, were nothing out of the way for the time. From one end of France to the other the touchy susceptibility of the nobles caused the most painful incidents ; so that at a moderate calculation the rage for duels cost more lives under the reigns of Henry III. and Henry IV. than ten years of civil war.

The captain's lodgings were furnished with taste. Embroidered silk curtains, and carpets of bright hue, at once caught the eyes of Mergy, who was accustomed to simpler fashions. He entered a small apartment which his brother called his oratory, the name of boudoir not having been yet invented. A faldstool of oak elaborately carved, a Madonna by an Italian master, and a holy-water stoup with its thick spray of box, seemed to justify the chamber's sacred designation; while a sofa covered in black damask, a mirror of Venice glass, a portrait of a lady, weapons, and musical instruments, suggested that the inmate was not unaccustomed to occupations something mundane in character.

Mergy cast a contemptuous eye on the holy-water stoup and its sprig, which reminded him disagreeably of his brother's apostasy. A lackey boy brought preserves, sweetmeats, and white wine; for tea and coffee were not yet in use, and the simple tastes of our ancestors put up with wine in the place of all such modish drinks.

Mergy, glass in hand, still kept looking from the Madonna to the stoup, and from the stoup to the faldstool. He sighed deeply; and gazing at his brother, who had stretched himself with a nonchalant air on the couch, he said, " Your Popish equipment is complete. What would our mother say if she were here ? "

The notion seemed to pain the captain. He bent his bushy eyebrows, and waved his hand as if to ask his brother not to broach such a subject; but Mergy went on pitilessly :

" Can you possibly have abjured our family faith with your heart as you have with your lips ? "

"Our family faith? it was never mine! What? *I* believe in the canting sermons that your ministers twang through their noses? *I——*"

"And it is better of course to believe in purgatory, in confession, in the infallibility of the Pope? It is better to throw oneself before the dusty sandals of a Capuchin? The time will come when you will think you cannot dine without gabbling the Baron de Vaudreuil's grace."

"Listen to me, Bernard. I hate argument, especially religious argument; but

I must have an explanation or later, and since we have I will speak to you without

with you sooner begun let us finish. concealment."

"Then you do not believe in the absurd inventions of the Papists?"

The captain shrugged his shoulders, and let one of his large spurs ring again as he dropped his heel on the floor. "Papists?" he cried, "Huguenots? What is there on either side but superstition? I cannot believe what reason shows me to be absurd. Our litanies and your psalms are both nonsense; one as bad as the other. Only," he added, smiling, "there is sometimes good music in our churches, while you wage immortal war with ears of taste."

"A pretty advantage for your religion, and a good reason for making proselytes to it!"

"Do not call it my religion, for I believe in it no more than in yours. Since I could think for myself, since my reason has been left uncontrolled——"

"But——"

"A truce with preachments. I know by heart everything that you can say to me. I too have had my hopes and my fears. Do you think I have not striven my utmost to keep the happy superstitions of childhood? I have read all the divines to find solace for the doubts that frightened me, and I but made them stronger. In short, I could not and I cannot believe. The precious gift of faith has been refused me, but I would not for the world deprive others of it."

"I am sorry for you."

"There, you are right enough. As a Protestant I did not believe in meeting; as a Catholic I do not believe any more in the mass. Are not the savageries of our civil wars enough, in God's name, to uproot the strongest faith?"

"But they are the work of men only, and of men who have perverted the word of God."

"That answer is not original; but you must not complain

if I am still unconvinced. I do not and I cannot comprehend your Deity ; and if I did believe, it would be, as our friend Jodelle says, ' with all rights reserved.'"

" But if the two faiths are indifferent to you, why that abjuration which has hurt your family and your friends so much ?"

" I have written at least a score of times to my father to explain my reasons to him and excuse myself ; but he has thrown my letters unopened into the fire, and has behaved to me more harshly than if I had committed some great crime."

" Neither my mother nor I approved this excessive sternness of his ; and if we had not received positive orders——"

" I do not know what has been thought of me, and I do not much care ; but I will tell you what made me take a sudden step, which, no doubt, I should not take if the thing were to be done afresh."

" Ah ! I always thought you would repent of it."

" Repent of it ? No ; for I do not think that I did ill. When you were still at school, busy with Latin and Greek, I had harness on back, had donned the white scarf,[1] and was fighting in our first civil war. Your little Prince of Condé, who was responsible for so many of your faction's faults— your Prince of Condé, I say, used to mind your business when his gallantries gave him time. A lady loved me and the prince wanted me to give her up to him ; I refused, and he became my mortal enemy. So he set himself to inflict on me all possible mortifications. ' The pretty little prince who is always kissing his ladylove ' pointed me out to the extremists of the party as a monster of debauchery and irreligion. Now I had but one mistress, and I clave to her.

---

[1] The reformers had chosen this party colour.

K

As for irreligion, I let others alone, why should they pick a quarrel with me ? "

" I should have thought it impossible that the prince could behave so ill."

" He is dead, and you have made a hero of him, which is the way of the world. He was not without merits. He died like a brave man, and I have forgiven him. But at that time he was all-powerful, and resistance on the part of a poor gentleman like me seemed to him a crime."

The captain paced the chamber for some time, and then continued in a voice of ever-increasing passion :

" Every minister, every fanatic in the army was soon set upon me. I cared as little for their snarling as for their sermons ; but one of the prince's gentlemen, to curry favour with his master, called me ' Lecher ' before all our captains. I boxed his ears first, and killed him afterwards. There were at least a dozen duels a day in the army, and our generals turned blind eyes to them. But *I* was made an exception ; and the prince determined that I should be a lesson to the whole army. The entreaties of all the men of quality—including, I must own, the Admiral—obtained my pardon ; but the prince's hatred was not satisfied. At Jazeneuil fight I was in command of a company of pistoliers ; I had been in the front of the melée ; two musket-ball dents in my cuirass and a lance-wound through my left arm showed that I had not spared myself. I had twenty men left, and a full battalion of the King's Swiss was marching on us. The Prince of Condé bade me charge them ; I asked him for two companies of Reiters, and—he called me a coward ! ' "

Mergy started up and seized his brother's hand. But the captain continued, still pacing up and down with eyes flashing fury.

"He called me coward before all these gentry in their gilded armour, who a few months afterwards deserted him and left him to be killed at Jarnac. I felt that there was nothing to do but to die. I dashed at the Swiss, swearing that if by any chance I came off with my life, I would never draw sword again for so unjust a prince. Wounded severely and unhorsed, I was on the point of being killed, when one of the Duke of Anjou's gentlemen, Béville, the same madcap with whom we dined to-day, saved my life, and introduced me to the duke. I was well treated, and I was thirsting for revenge. They made much of me; they urged me to take service with my benefactor the duke; they quoted the line—

"Omne solum forti patria est, ut piscibus æquor."

I was disgusted at the Protestants for calling foreigners into our country. But why not confess the one true reason which actuated me? I longed for vengeance, and I turned Catholic in hopes of meeting the Prince of Condé on the battle-field and killing him. A coward undertook the business of paying my debts; and the way in which he was killed almost made me forget my hatred. I saw him a bleeding prey to the soldiers' insults: I rescued his corpse from their hands, and flung my own mantle over it. But I was already pledged to the Catholics: I had a troop in their cavalry, and I could not leave them. Luckily, I think I may say I have been of some service to my old side: I tried whenever I could to soften the rage of a religious war, and I was fortunate enough to save the lives of some old friends."

"Oliver de Basseviile tells everyone that he owes his life to you."

"So I am a Catholic now," said George in a calmer tone. "It is as good a religion as any other; for it is so easy to get on with their pious people. You see that pretty Madonna? 'Tis the portrait of an Italian courtesan; and yet fanatics admire my piety, while they cross themselves before her virginship. I warrant you I have an easier time with them than with our ministers. I can live as I please at the cost of a very few sacrifices to the prejudices of the vulgar. One must go to mass: I go now and then—to look at the pretty women. One must have a confessor: well, mine is a Franciscan, a capital fellow, who has been a horse arquebusier, and who for a crown gives me my confession ticket, and carries my own billets to his pretty penitents into the bargain. Death of my life! the mass for ever!"

Mergy could not help smiling.

"Here," went on the captain, "is my Church Service,"

and he threw him a book richly bound in velvet cover and silver clasps; "these 'Hours' are well worth your Prayer-books."

Mergy read on the back, "Hours of the Court."

"It is a pretty binding," said he scornfully, handing the book back.

The captain opened it, and returned it again with a smile. Mergy read on the title-page, "The Very Horrific Life of the Great Gargantua, Father of Pantagruel. Composed by Master Alcofribas, Extractor of Quintessence."

"That is the book for me," cried the captain laughing. "I rate it higher than all the divinity books in the Geneva Library."

"They say, no doubt, that the author was learned enough, but he has hardly made a good use of his learning."

George shrugged his shoulders.

"Read it, Bernard, and you shall tell me what you think of it afterwards."

Mergy took the book, but after a moment's silence :

"I am still sorry," said he, "that mere disgust, however well-founded, should have drawn you into a step which you will certainly repent some day."

The captain's head sank, and his eyes appeared to be carefully tracing the pattern of the carpet at his feet. "What is done is done," said he, smothering a sigh. "Perhaps," he added in a gayer tone, "I shall come back to meeting some day. But meanwhile let us drop the subject : promise me never to return to one so tiresome."

"I hope your own conscience will do more than my lectures or my advice."

"Be it so. And now let us talk of *your* business. What was your object in coming to Court ?"

"I hope for strong enough recommendations to the
Admiral to obtain admission for me among his gentlemen in
the campaign he is going to make in the Netherlands."

"I do not like your plan. No gentleman who has a good
heart in his breast and a sword by his side ought of his own
free will to make a lackey of himself. Volunteer for the
Royal Guards; for my own company of light horse, if you
like. You will make the campaign, as we all shall, under
the Admiral's orders; but at least you will be no one's
body-servant."

"But I have no desire to join the King's Guard; I had
even much rather not. It would please me well enough to
serve in your company; but my father wishes me to make
my first campaign under the Admiral's immediate leading."

"That is like you Huguenot gentry. You preach union,
and yet you bear old grudges worse than we do ours."

"How so?"

"Why, you still look on the King as a tyrant, an 'Ahab,'
as your ministers call him. Nay, he is not even your king;
he is an usurper; and since the death of Louis XIII.,[1] 'tis
Gaspard I. who is King of France."

"That is an idle jest."

"Well, well; you may as well serve old Gaspard as the
Duke of Guise; for M. de Châtillon is really a great captain,
and you will learn your trade under him."

"So even his enemies esteem him," said Mergy.

"Hum! A certain pistol-shot was not quite to his credit."

"He has proved his innocence; and besides, his whole
life is utterly out of harmony with Poltrot's cowardly crime."

[1] Prince Louis of Condé, who was killed at Jarnac, was accused by the
Catholics of having designs on the crown. Admiral Coligny's name was
Gaspard.

" Yet," said George, "you know the Latin axiom, ' He whom it profited did it.' Without that pistol-shot Orleans would have fallen."

" But after all, it was only a man the less in the Catholic army."

" Yes, but what a man ! Did you never hear two lines—bad verse enough, but as good as your psalms—

> " For so many Guisards as keep the dance,
> So many Mérés are still in France." [1]

" Idle threats, and nothing more," answered Mergy. " It would be a long list if I were to run over all the crimes of the Guisards themselves."

" As for me, if I were King of France, this is what I would do to restore peace. I would stow Guises and Châtillons both in a good leathern bag, well sewn and well tied up, and I would throw them into the sea with a thousand quintals of iron for ballast, that not a soul might escape. I could find room in the bag for some other folk too."

" It is lucky, then, that you are not King of France."

After this, the conversation took a livelier turn, politics and theology both being dropped : and the brothers told all the little matters that had happened to them since they parted. Mergy frankly told against himself the story of the Lion d'Or ; and his brother, laughing heartily at it, joked him not a little on the loss of his eighteen crowns and his good chestnut. But the bells of a neighbouring church broke in on the talk.

[1] Poltrot de Méré, who murdered the great Duke Francis of Guise at the siege of Orleans, just as the town was at the last extremity. Coligny justified himself, not too successfully, from the charge of having allowed, or not prevented, the crime.

"*Parbleu!*" said the captain. "Come to church this evening! I am sure it will amuse you."

"Thank you, but I feel no desire to be converted yet."

"Do come: to-day's preacher is Brother Lubin, a cordelier who makes religion such a joke that crowds flock to

hear him. Besides, the whole Court is going to St. Jacques to day: 'tis a sight to see."

"And will Madame de Turgis be there? and will she take her mask off?"

"Why, certainly: she is bound to be there. If you want

to enter your name for the stake, do not forget when church is over to wait at the door and offer her holy water. That is another of the admirable ceremonies of the Catholic Church. Heavens! how many pretty hands I have squeezed! how many billets-doux I have slipped in, while giving this same holy water!"

"Somehow it is so disgusting to me, that I do not think anything in the world would induce me to dip my finger in it."

But the captain interrupted him with a shout of laughter; and both, having cloaked themselves, made for the church of St. Jacques, where a fair and numerous company was already assembled.

L

CHAPTER V.

THE SERMON.

"With mouth well open, a fine de-
spatcher of Hours, good at driving
through a Mass, good at polishing off
Vigils; and to put the whole shortly,
a true monk if ever there
was one since a monking
world monked its monkery."
RABELAIS.

A S Captain George
and his brother
crossed the church to find
a comfortable place near
the preacher, their atten-
tion was caught by bursts of laughter coming from the
sacristy; and going in thither, they found a fat man, with a

cheerful and florid countenance, clothed in the gown of
St. Francis, and conversing in a very lively manner with
half-a-dozen splendidly dressed young men.

"Come, children," said he, "be quick. The ladies are
tired of waiting. Give me my text."

"Talk of the tricks these same ladies play their husbands," quoth one of the young men, whom George recognized at once as Béville.

"I grant you the subject is fertile, my boy; but what can
I say so good as the sermon of the Pontoise preacher who
cried: 'I am going to throw my cap at the head of that
woman among you who has planted her husband's brows
thickest with horns'; whereat there was not a wife in the
church who did not shield her head with arm or mantle, as
if to ward off the blow."

"Oh, Father Lubin," said another, "I only came to
sermon for your sake! Prithee give us something merry
to-day. Talk of love. It is a sin which is fashionable
enough now."

"Fashionable, you call it? Fashionable for you gentlemen who are twenty-five; but I am well into my fifties.
At my age one cannot talk of love; and for my part I have
forgotten what the sin means."

"Don't make a prim mouth, Father Lubin. You can
talk about it just as well as ever. We know you."

"Yes," added Béville. "Preach on Luxury. The ladies
will all say that you are very full of your subject."

To which jest the cordelier replied with a sly wink,
showing both the pride and the pleasure he felt at being
upbraided with a young man's vice.

"No, I will not preach about it; because the Court dames
would have no more of me for confessor if I showed myself

too severe on that score : and in conscience, if I spoke at
all on it, it would be to show how men risk their eternal
welfare—for what?—for a single minute of pleasure!"

"Well then—But here is the captain. Come, George,
give us a text. Father Lubin has promised to preach on
the first subject we give him."

"Yes," said the monk. "But death of my life! be quick.
I ought to be in the pulpit by this time."

"Why, Father Lubin, you swear as well as the King
could do!" cried George.

"I bet he will not swear in his sermon," said Béville.

"Why not, if the fancy takes me?" answered Father
Lubin boldly.

"I bet ten pistoles that you will not dare."

"Ten pistoles?—Done!"

"I will go shares with you, Béville," said the captain.

"No, no!" said he. "I will have the good father's
money all to myself: and if he swears, faith! I shall not
regret my own. Oaths from a preacher are quite worth ten
pistoles."

"And I tell you that the money is mine," said Father
Lubin. "I will begin my sermon with three oaths. Ah,
my good young gentlemen, because you wear sword at side
and plume in hat, you think you alone know how to swear.
We shall see."

And so speaking he went out of the sacristy and mounted
the pulpit. Forthwith a deep silence fell on the assembly.

The preacher ran his eyes over the crowd that thronged
round the pulpit, as if to find out the layer of the bet : and
descrying him leaning against a pillar immediately in front,
he bent his brows, set fist on hip, and in the tone of an
angry man began thus :

" My dear brethren, by the virtue ! by the death ! by the
blood !———"

A murmur of indignant surprise interrupted him, or
rather filled the pause which he designedly made.

"——of God," continued the Franciscan, with the most pious
twang possible, " we are saved and delivered from hell."

A roar of general laughter interrupted him for the second
time ; and Béville, taking his purse from his girdle, shook it
ostentatiously before the preacher as an admission that he
had lost.

" Well, my brethren," continued the unruffled father,
" you think it is all right, do you not ?   ' We are saved and
delivered from hell.'   These are comfortable words, think
you ?   We can fold our arms and take our ease.   We have
got rid of those nasty hell-flames.   As for purgatory-fire, it
is only as it were a singeing with a taper, to be cured by
oil of masses—a dozen at most.   Come, let us eat, let us
drink, let us go and see Polly and Dolly.   This is how
you reckon, hardened sinners that you are.   Now I, Brother
Lubin—I tell you that you reckon without your host !

" You, for instance, you heretical gentry, you Huguenots
of the Huguenots, you think that it was to deliver *you* from
hell that our Saviour deigned to let Himself be crucified ?
Fools !   It is very likely, is it not, that He should have shed
His precious blood for rascals like you ?   That would have
been (not to speak irreverently) throwing pearls to swine,
and our Saviour's way was the other—to throw swine to
pearls, for there are pearls in the sea, and our Lord threw
into the sea two thousand swine.   And ' Behold, the whole
herd ran violently down a steep place into the sea.'   A good
journey to you, my masters the pigs ! and may all heretics
go the same way !"

The speaker coughed, and stopped a minute to see and
enjoy the effect of his eloquence on the
faithful ; then he went on :

"Therefore, ye Huguenots, be converted, and be quick about it, or else
woe to you! You are
neither saved nor de-
livered from hell, so
show a clean pair of
heels to meeting,
and cry 'The mass
for ever!'

"But you, my dear
Catholic brethren,
you rub your hands
and lick your lips,

thinking you are in the pleasant suburbs of Paradise already. To speak frankly, my brethren, it is farther from the Court where you dwell to Paradise (even if you take the short cut across) than it is from Saint Lazare to the Porte St. Denis.

" ' The virtue, the death, the blood of God have saved you and delivered you from hell.' Yes, I grant you, by freeing you from the burden of original sin. But woe to you if Satan catches you up again. And I tell you that he goeth about seeking whom he may devour. Oh, my dear brethren, Satan is one who could teach a trick or two of fence to Big John, Little John, and the Englishman himself : and I tell you of a truth, fierce are the attacks he makes on us.

" For as soon as we doff our petticoats, and are breeched —as soon, I say, as we are in case to be guilty of mortal sin—Master Satan challenges us to the Pré-aux-Clercs of this life. Our arms are the holy sacraments : as for him, he has a whole arsenal of weapons, to wit, our sins, which supply him with arms of offence and defence at once.

" I can see him coming on the ground : his cuirass of *gluttony* on his body, his spurs of *idleness* at his heels, the long sword of *luxury* at his girdle. His dagger is *envy*, he wears *pride* on his head as a man-at-arms wears his morion ; he has *avarice* in his pocket to use at need ; and *anger*, with insults, and all that follow them, he holds in his mouth :— whence it will be clear to you that he is literally armed to the teeth.

" When God has given the word, Satan does not, like our punctilious duellists, say, ' Sir, are you ready ?' but plunges headlong on the Christian without crying, ' Ware !' But the Christian, seeing that he is going to receive a thrust from *gluttony* in the belly, parries with *fasting*."

Here the preacher, to make his discourse clearer, took a crucifix, and began to fence with it, lunging and parrying exactly as a fencing-master would use a foil to illustrate a difficult stroke.

"Satan, in the very act of recovery, puts in a cut of *anger*, and then, feinting with *hypocrisy*, thrusts in quart with *pride*. The Christian first protects himself with *patience*, and then replies to *pride* with a lunge from *humility*. Satan, angry at this, tries at once a resolute stoccata with *luxury*, but perceiving it to be parried with *mortification*, he throws himself recklessly on his foe, trying to trip up his heels with *idleness*, and at the same time aiming a dagger blow of *envy* at him, while he tries to slip *avarice* into his heart. Then is there need of a firm foot and a quick eye. With *labour* the trick of *idleness* is foiled; the dagger of *envy* is blunted by *love-of-our-neighbour* (not an easy parry, my friends); and as for the privy thrust of *avarice*, nothing but *charity* can ward off that.

"But, my brethren, how many of you are there who, when attacked thus in tierce and in quart, with cut and with thrust, would be ever ready with a parry for every pass of the Enemy? Many a champion have I seen beat to the ground: and then, if he has not swift recourse to *contrition*, he is a lost man; and you cannot be too quick in using this last resort. You think, you courtiers, that *Peccavi* is a short word to say. Alas! my brethren, how many poor dying sinners try to say it and their voice fails them at the *Pec!* And then, presto! there is a soul carried off by the devil! Fetch it back who can."

Brother Lubin continued his eloquent harangue for some considerable time; and when he came down the pulpit steps a connoisseur in style observed, that though he had preached barely an hour, his discourse made thirty-seven distinct points, besides flashes of wit (such as those I have quoted) which no man could number. Catholics and Protestants joined in applauding the preacher, who was long detained at the foot of the pulpit by an eager crowd pressing from all parts of the church to congratulate him.

During the sermon Mergy had several times asked where Madame de Turgis was ; and his brother had looked for her in vain. Either the fair countess was not in church, or she had hidden herself from admiration in some dark corner.

" I wish," said Mergy as he went out, " that all who were present at this absurd sermon could this moment hear one of the simple exhortations of our ministers."

" There she is !" said the captain, whispering and pressing his arm.

Mergy turned his head, and saw, passing like lightning through the dark doorway, a lady magnificently dressed, and conducted by a young man of fair complexion and small stature, slight in figure, effeminate in air, and dressed with probably studied carelessness. The crowd made way for them with a readiness that savoured of alarm ; for the cavalier was the redoubted Comminges.

Mergy had scarce time to glance at the countess. He could not even distinctly see her features, though they made a great impression on him as a whole. But to Comminges he had taken a mortal dislike, though at the same time without quite knowing why. He was indignant at seeing such an insignificant appearance coupled with such a repu- tation. " If the countess," he thought, " loved anyone in this crowd, that monster Comminges would kill him. He has sworn to kill all whom she loves," and he grasped the hilt of his sword with an involuntary and excited movement of which he was at once ashamed. " What does it matter to me, after all? I have hardly seen his conquest, and do not grudge her to him." But his thoughts had left a disagreeable impression, and he did not speak from the church to the captain's house.

They found supper on table; but Mergy ate little, and as soon as the cloth was removed expressed a wish to return to his inn. The captain made no objection to his going, on condition that he would next day come and take up his quarters definitely.

We need not say that Mergy was supplied by his brother with money, a horse, and so forth; together with the address of the court tailor, and of the only shop where a gentleman who was anxious to stand well with the ladies could buy his gloves, his ruffs *à la confusion*, and his shoes *à cric* or *à pont-levis*.

At last, darkness having set in, he returned to his inn, accompanied by two of his brother's serving-men well armed with sword and pistol; for the streets of Paris after eight o'clock were more dangerous then than the road from Seville to Granada is now.

CHAPTER VI.

A PARTY LEADER.

"Jockey of Norfolk, be not too bold !
For Dickon thy master is bought and sold."
SHAKESPEARE, *King Richard III.*

WHEN Bernard de Mergy returned to his modest hostelry he glanced in a melancholy manner at the worn and tarnished furniture. As he silently compared the walls, once whitewashed, now blackened with smoke, to the bright silken tapestries of the lodging he had just quitted— as he remembered the beautiful painting of the Madonna, and saw nothing on his own walls but an old image of a saint, a base enough thought entered his mind. All that luxury, all that elegance, the good graces of ladies, the King's favour—all these desirable things had cost George but a word, a single word, easy enough to pronounce, for it had to come from the lips only, and no question was asked about the heart. At the same time, there occurred to him the names of divers Protestants who, by abjuration, had raised themselves to the highest honours; and as the devil makes strings to his bow out of anything, the parable of the Prodigal Son also suggested itself, but with this moral, foreign to the original, that there would be more joy over a converted Huguenot than over a consistent Catholic.

These thoughts, which recurred in divers shapes, and as it were independently of his will, haunted him constantly, despite his disgust at them. He took a Geneva Bible which had belonged to his mother, and read it for some time, until, calmed at length, he laid the book down, and, before he closed his eyes, swore to himself to live and die in the faith of his fathers.

Yet notwithstanding his reading and his oath, his dreams showed the impress of the day's adventures. He had visions of curtains of purple silk, of golden plate: and then suddenly the tables were upset, swords flashed, and blood mingled with the wine. Again, the painted Madonna became alive; she left her frame and danced before him. He tried to register her features in his memory; and only then noticed that she was masked in black. But ah! the dark blue eyes and the glimpse of white skin that shone through the opening of the mask! Next, the mask-strings fell, and a face appeared—a face of heavenly beauty, but still without clearly distinguishable traits, like the reflection of a nymph in troubled water. Against his will his eyes drooped; but he raised them quickly, and had before him only the redoubtable Comminges, a bloody sword in his hand.

He rose early, caused his slender baggage to be carried to his brother's house, and, declining George's offer to show him the sights of the town, went by himself to the Hotel de Châtillon to present to the Admiral the letters with which his father had charged him.

He found the courtyard of the hotel thronged with servants and horses, and had some trouble in making his way through these to a large ante-room filled with squires and pages, who, though only armed with their swords, made up an imposing body-guard around the Admiral. An usher in black garments, after a glance at Mergy's lace collar and at a gold chain which his brother had lent him, made no difficulty in admitting him at once to the gallery where his master was.

The Admiral was surrounded by nobles, gentlemen, and ministers of the gospel, to the number of more than forty —all standing with uncovered head and respectful attitude. He was very simply dressed in a complete suit of black. His stature was lofty, but slightly bowed, and his bald forehead was wrinkled rather by the toils of war than by years. A long white beard fell upon his breast. His cheeks, naturally hollow, appeared even more so, thanks to a wound, the deep scar of which was hardly hidden by his long moustache; for a pistol-ball at Montcontour had pierced his cheek and broken several teeth. His countenance was sad rather than severe, and men said that since the brave Dandelot's [1] death none had seen him smile. He stood with his hand resting on a table covered with maps and plans, among which towered a huge quarto Bible; while toothpicks scattered among the charts and papers bore witness to a habit which was often made the subject of jest. A secretary, seated at one end of the table, seemed hard at work writing letters, which he afterwards presented to the Admiral for signature.

[1] His brother.

At the sight of the great man, who, in the eyes of his co-religionists, was more than a king—uniting in his own person both hero and saint— Mergy felt so much veneration, that in presenting himself he, without intending it, bent one knee to the ground. The Admiral, surprised and vexed at this unusual mark of respect, signed to him to rise, and took the letter which the young enthusiast held out with a slight touch of impatience. Then, glancing at the arms on the seal, " It is," he said, " from my old comrade, the Baron de Mergy ; and you, young man, are so like him, that you must be his son."

" Sir, my father would gladly, had his great age permitted, have made the journey himself to pay his respects to you."

"Gentlemen," said Coligny, turning to those about him after he had read the letter, " I present to you the son of the Baron de Mergy, who has come two hundred leagues and more to join us. We shall have no lack, it seems, of volunteers for Flanders. Gentlemen, I ask your friendship for the son ; you already know the high worth of the father."

And Mergy at once received a score of embraces and offers of assistance. " Are you a soldier already, my friend Bernard ?" asked the Admiral : " have you ever heard a shot fired ?"

Mergy blushed as he answered that he had not yet had the good luck to fight for the religion.

" Congratulate yourself rather, young man," said Coligny, gravely, " that you have not yet been obliged to shed your countrymen's blood. Thank God ! " he added sighing, "civil war is over, the religion has a breathing time, and you, happier than we were, will only draw sword against the foes of your king and country." Then, putting his hand on the young man's shoulder, "I am sure," said he, "you will not belie the race from which you spring. As your father wishes, you shall serve first among my gentlemen; and when we meet the Spaniards, capture one of their standards, and you shall have a cornetcy in my regiment on the spot."

"Then I swear," cried Mergy resolvedly, "that at the first action I will be a cornet or my father shall lose a son."

"Well said, brave boy! You speak like your father;" and he called his steward. "This," he said, "is my steward, Master Samuel. If you want money for outfit, talk to him."

The steward bowed to Mergy, who quickly returned his thanks, but declined the kindness. "My father and my brother," he said, "have supplied my wants amply."

"Your brother? Is that Captain George Mergy, who, at the first war, abjured his faith?"

Mergy dropped his head sadly; and though his lips moved his reply was inaudible.

"'Tis a brave soldier," went on the Admiral; "but what is courage without the fear of God? Young man, you have in your family an example to shun as well as a pattern to follow."

"I will try to imitate my brother's brave deeds, and not his perversion."

"Well then, Bernard, come and see me often, and count

N

on me as your friend. The city you are in is no good school
of morals; but I hope to carry you soon where there will
be glory to earn."

Mergy bowed respectfully, and fell back into the circle
which surrounded the Admiral.

"Gentlemen," said Coligny, resuming the conversation
which Mergy's entrance had interrupted, "I hear good news
from all sides. The assassins at Rouen have been punished."

"But not those at Toulouse," said an old minister of
gloomy and fanatic aspect.

"You mistake, sir; I have just heard the news of their
punishment. Moreover, the mixed commission [1] is already
appointed at Toulouse. Every day his majesty gives proof
that his justice is equal for all."

The old minister shook his head doubtingly, and another
greybeard, clothed in black velvet, cried, "His justice is
equal! Yes: Charles and his worthy mother would like to
strike all down—Châtillons, Montmorencys and Guises all
together—with a single blow."

"Speak more respectfully of your King, M. de Bonissan,"
said Coligny sternly. "Let us, I pray you, at last forget our
old grudges. Give none cause to say that the Catholics
practise better than we do the divine precept of forgetful-
ness of injuries."

"By the bones of my father!" muttered Bonissan, "they
have the easier task! My memory does not so easily let
slip twenty-three martyrs of my kin."

He was speaking thus bitterly when an old and broken-

---

[1] By the treaty which ended the third civil war, chambers of justice had
been established in several provincial parliaments, half of whose members
professed Protestantism. These chambers were to try causes between Protestants and Catholics.

looking man, of repulsive aspect, wrapped in a worn grey mantle, entered the gallery, threaded the press, and gave a sealed paper to Coligny.

" Who are you ? " said the Admiral, without breaking the seal.

" A friend," replied the old man hoarsely ; and he left the room at once.

" I saw that man come out of the Hotel de Guise this very morning," said one gentleman.

" He is a wizard," said another.

" A poisoner," cried a third.

" The Duke of Guise has sent him to poison the Admiral."

" To poison me ? " cried Coligny shrugging his shoulders. " To poison me in a letter ! "

" Have you forgotten the Queen of Navarre's gloves ?"[1] cried Bonissan.

" I no more believe in the poisoned gloves than in the poisoned letter ; but I do believe that the Duke of Guise is incapable of such baseness."

He was about to open the letter, when Bonissan flung himself upon him, and seized his hands, crying—

" Do not unseal it, or you will inhale some mortal odour."

All the company crowded round the Admiral, who strove to get rid of Bonissan.

" I see a black vapour arising from the letter ! " cried one. And the general cry was, " Throw it away ! "

" Unhand me, madmen ! " said the Admiral struggling ; and as they wrestled with him the paper fell on the floor.

---

[1] " Her death," says D'Aubigné, " was caused by poison, communicated to the brain by perfumed gloves of the manufacture of Messer René the Florentine, a wretch since execrated even by the Queen's enemies."— *Hist. Univ*, II. ii.

" Samuel, my good fellow," cried Bonissan, " show yourself a faithful servant. Open the packet, and do not give it
to your master till you are sure that
there is nothing wrong with it."

The commission did not seem to
be to the steward's taste;
but Mergy, without hesi-
tating, picked up the
letter and broke the seal.
The circle at once fell
widely away from him,
each man retiring as if
a mine were about to be
sprung in the
middle of the
room. Yet
no evil va-
pour came

forth, and no
one even
sneezed. Some
rather dirty
paper, with a few lines of writing
on it, formed the sole contents of the terrible packet. And
the same individuals who had been the first to retire were
also the first to come forward with smiling faces as soon as
all appearance of danger had vanished.

" What means this insolence ? " cried Coligny angrily, as
he freed himself at length from Bonissan's grasp. " Open
a letter addressed to me !"

" My Lord Admiral, if it had happened that this letter contained any poison subtle enough to kill by inhalation, it were better that a youth like myself fell victim, than you whose life is so precious to the religion."

A murmur of admiration rose around him. Coligny pressed his hand with much feeling, and after a moment's silence said kindly—

" As you have done the deed of unsealing this letter, read us the contents."

Mergy at once read as follows :

" The western sky glows with bloody light. Stars have fallen from the firmament, and flaming swords have been seen in the air. All but blind men must perceive what these things portend. Gaspard ! buckle on sword and spur, or in a few days' time the gleds shall glut themselves with thy flesh."

" By the ' gleds ' he means the Guises !" said Bonissan. " G for G." [1]

The Admiral raised his shoulders disdainfully, and no one spoke ; but it was clear that the prophecy had made a certain impression on the company.

" There be many folk," said Coligny coolly, " at Paris who busy themselves with folly. Do not men say that there are some ten thousand rascals here who live by fortune-telling ? "

" The warning, such as it is, is not to be despised," said a captain of infantry. " The Duke of Guise has said openly

---

[1] It was necessary to be unfaithful here, the play on *gai* (" jay," not exactly " gled " or " kite,") and the letter *g* as pronounced in French, being unmanageable in English I have therefore changed the bird, and paraphrased Bonissan's " le nom d'un oiseau est mis là au lieu de la lettre qui se prononce de méme.")—*Translator's note.*

enough that he shall never sleep sound till he has passed
his sword through your body."

"It is so easy," added Bonissan, "for an assassin to obtain
admission to you! Were I in your place, I would never
go to the Louvre without a corslet on."

"Go to, comrade," said the Admiral. "It is not with old
soldiers like us that assassins meddle : they fear us more
than we fear them."

He talked for some time longer about the Flanders
campaign and the affairs of the religion. Divers persons
brought him petitions to present to the King, and he received them all kindly, addressing some affable remark to
each suitor. At length, as ten o'clock struck, he called for
his hat and gloves, to go to the Louvre, and some of the
company took leave : but the greater number went with
him, to serve at once as suite and escort.

CHAPTER VII.

THE captain had no sooner caught sight of his brother than he cried out—

"Well, have you seen Gaspard the First? How did he receive you?"

"With kindness that I shall never forget."

"I am very glad of it."

"Oh, George, what a man!"

"What a man? I take it he is a man much like the rest of us; with, let us say, a little more ambition and a little

more faculty of endurance than my footman, not to mention
the difference of their origin. M. de Châtillon's birth has
done something for him."

" Did his birth teach him the art of war or make him the
first captain of our time ? "

"Why no : though his proficiency in that respect has
not saved him from being always beaten. But there, let
us talk of something else. You have seen the Admiral
to-day : 'tis very well. Give every man his due of honour :
and you had to begin by paying your respects to M. de
Châtillon. Now, will you come and hunt to-morrow ? If
you will, I will introduce you there to someone who
is also worth knowing ; that is to say, Charles, King of
France."

"What ! You wish me to go to the royal hunt ? "

" I do : and you shall there see the prettiest ladies as well
as the finest horses of the Court. The meet is at the
Château de Madrid, and we must be there early to-morrow
morning. I will give you my dapple grey, and I warrant
you there will be no need of spurring to keep up with the
hounds."

At this moment a lackey gave Mergy a letter, which one
of the King's pages had just brought. Mergy opened it,
and his brother's surprise equalled his own when they found
enclosed a cornet's commission, drawn up in regular form,
and with the King's seal attached.

" Plague take us !" said George ; " here is a prompt mark
of favour ! But why the devil does Charles IX., who is
not aware of your existence, send you a cornet's commission ?"

" I think," said Mergy, "that I owe it to the Admiral."
And he told his brother the story of the mysterious letter

in opening which he had shown so much courage. The captain laughed consumedly at the end of the adventure, and rallied him on it without mercy.

CHAPTER VIII.

"AH! Mr. Author, what an opportunity have you here of drawing portraits—and such portraits! You are going to take us to the Château de Madrid, in the midst of the Court—and such a Court! Will you exhibit it thoroughly to us, French-Italian as it was? Will you pass all its notables, one after the other, before us? How much we shall learn, and how interesting a day spent among so many great personages will be!"

" Alas ! master reader, what is this that you ask ? I wish
I had the talent for writing a history of France : in that case
I should not spend my time in writing romances. But tell
me why you wish me to introduce you to people who have
no part to play in my story ?"

" But it is a shame of you not to make them play a part
in it ! You drag me off to the year 1572, and then you
want to sneak out of giving the portraits of all these great
men. Come, come, no shilly-shallying ; begin at once. I
will tell you how : ' *The door of the withdrawing room
opened, and there appeared*——' "

" But, good reader, there were no withdrawing rooms at
the Château de Madrid. *Salons* only began——"

" Well, well—then : ' *The great hall was crowded, and
among others might have been perceived*——' "

" Perhaps you will be good enough to say who ?"

" Why, of course, Charles IX. in the first place."

" And in the second ?"

" Soft : not so fast. Tell me first what the King wore ;
then sketch his person, and then his character. That is the
regular path that every novelist has to tread nowadays."

" What he wore ? It was a hunting dress, with a great
horn slung round his neck."

" You are laconic."

" As for his looks, let us see——it would be much better
for you to go and see his bust at the Angoulême Museum,
Room 2, Number 98."

" But, good Mr. Author, I live in the country ; and would
you make me come to Paris on purpose to see a bust of
Charles IX. ?"

" Well then, imagine a young man fairly well made, but
with his head set somewhat deep between his shoulders. His

neck is stretched out, and his forehead leans
forward in an awkward fashion; his nose is
rather thick, his lips are thin and long, and
the upper one protrudes; his complexion is
pale, and his large greenish eyes never look
his interlocutor in the face. But you will not
see 'Saint Bartholomew,' or anything like
it, written in his glance. Far from
it: his expression is only rather
stupid and wistful, not harsh or
ferocious. You may
picture it well enough
by fancying a young
Englishman who
makes his ap-
pearance in a
large drawing-
room where
everyone is sit-
ting down. He
walks through a
double row of
well-dressed women,
who are silent as he
passes; he entangles
himself with the
dress of one, jostles
another's chair, and has
the utmost difficulty in
reaching the lady of the
house. Then, and not till then,
he sees that in getting out of his carriage he has

CHARLES IX

muddied the sleeve of his coat against the wheel. You must
have seen faces aghast in this fashion; perhaps, indeed,

you may have seen your own reflected in some mirror before the
habit of going into society made
you indifferent to the effect of
your entrance———"

"And Catherine de Medicis?"

"Catherine de Medicis! Deuce
take me if I had so much as
thought of her. I think I shall
never have to mention her name
again; but if you must know, she
was a stout woman, well enough
preserved, as the saying is, with
a thick nose, and lips pinched
like those of a person who feels
the first approach of sea sickness.
Her eyes are half shut, she is
constantly yawning, and her voice
takes the same tone whether it
says, 'Who will rid me of that
hateful Bearnese woman?' or
'Madeleine, give my Naples lap-
dog some sugared cream.'"

"Good; but please put something more noteworthy in her
mouth. She has just (so they say)
had Jeanne d'Albret poisoned, and
there ought to be some sign of that."

"Not at all; for if any signs showed, what would become
of her famous power of dissimulation? Besides, if my

information is correct, she talked of nothing but the weather all that day."

"And Henry IV.? and Marguerite of Navarre? Show us Henry, the brave, gallant, kind Henry; show us Marguerite slipping a billet into a page's hand, while her husband, for his part, squeezes a maid of honour's fingers."

"As for Henry, no one could guess in that young featherhead the future hero and King of France. He has forgotten his mother, but a fortnight dead; and is talking to nobody but a pricker, with whom he holds endless converse about the slot of the stag who is about to be started. I will spare you that, especially as I hope you are no sportsman."

"And Marguerite?"

"She was not well that day, and kept her room."

"A neat way of getting rid of her! But the Duke of Anjou, and Condé, and Guise, and Tavannes, Retz, La Rochefoucauld, Téligny, Thoré, Méru, and all the rest?"

"You seem to know more about them than I do. I am going to talk about my friend Mergy."

"Sir, I am sorry to perceive that I shall not find what I sought in this story of yours."

"Really, I am very much afraid you will not."

GASPARD DE COLIGNY SEIGNEUR DE
CHATILLON

AMIRAL DE FRANCE

CHAPTER IX.

THE GLOVE.

" There fell a slipper [glove] from the right
hand of my Lady Blanche (from the left
it had been of no consequence), and made
Love let fly his shaft at the hidalgos."—LOPE
DE VEGA, *El guante de Doña Blanca.*

THE Court was at the Château de Madrid, and the
Queen-mother, surrounded by her ladies, was in her
chamber, expecting the King to come and breakfast with her
before getting in the saddle. The King himself, followed by
the princes, was slowly crossing a gallery where all the
gentlemen who were about to follow the hunt were assembled.

P

He listened with an inattentive air to the speeches which his courtiers made to him, frequently answering with abruptness. As he passed before the two brothers the captain bent one knee and presented the new cornet. Mergy, with a profound bow, thanked his majesty for the honour which he had received before doing anything to deserve it.

"Ah! you are he of whom my father the Admiral spoke. You are Captain George's brother?"

"Yes, sire."

"Are you Catholic or Huguenot?"

"I am a Protestant, sire."

"I but asked you for curiosity's sake. The devil take me if I care of what religion those are who serve me well." With which notable words the King turned into the Queen's apartments.

A few moments afterwards a bevy of ladies spread themselves about the gallery, seemingly sent to make the time appear less long to the intending riders. I shall mention but a single beauty in a Court fertile in beauties— the Countess de Turgis, who plays a great part in this story. She wore a riding-habit of a dashing and elegant fashion, and had not yet put on her mask. Her complexion, of dazzling whiteness, but tinged by no colour anywhere, set off her jet-black hair; and her arched eyebrows, just meeting in the midst, gave to her expression an air of hardness, or rather of pride, without destroying the attraction of her features as a whole. The first impression that her large blue eyes gave was one of haughty disdain; but when she talked with interest the pupils were soon seen to dilate like a cat's, her glance lighted up, and it was difficult even for a hardened coxcomb to resist their fascination for any length of time.

"Look at the Countess de Turgis! How beautiful she is to-day!" the courtiers muttered to each other, pressing forward to see her better. Mergy, who happened to be full in her path, was so struck with her beauty that he remained motionless, and had no thought of making way for her till the countess's wide silken sleeves touched his doublet.

She noticed his emotion, perhaps with pleasure, and deigned for a moment to fix her lovely eyes on his, which fell at once, while his cheeks reddened deeply. The countess smiled, and as she passed, she dropped one of her gloves in front of our hero, who, still entranced and motionless, never thought of picking it up. Immediately a fair young man (none other than Comminges), who happened to be behind Mergy, pushed rudely past him to seize the glove, which, after kissing it devoutly, he returned to Madame de Turgis. She did not thank him, but turned to Mergy, gazed at him for a time with an air of withering contempt, and then, noticing Captain George near him, "Captain," said she, "tell me where this tall simpleton comes from? to judge by his courtesy he must be some Huguenot."

A general burst of laughter at the remark completed the confusion of its unlucky object.

"'Tis my brother, lady," replied George, not quite so loud. "He has been at Paris but three days; and on my honour he is not more awkward than Lannoy was before you were good enough to take him in hand."

The countess blushed a little. "Captain," said she, "that is an unkind jest. Speak no ill of the dead. But give me your hand; I have a message to you from a lady who has somewhat to complain of you."

The captain took her hand ceremoniously, and conducted her to a window seat at some distance; but as she went she turned back once more to look at Mergy.

He, still dazzled by the beautiful apparition at which he burned to gaze, and to which he did not dare to lift his eyes, felt a gentle tap on his shoulder. Turning, he saw the Baron de Vaudreuil, who took his hand and led him aside, that they might, as he said, talk without fear of interruption.

"My dear friend," said the baron, "you are quite a new-comer in this region, and it is possible that you do not yet know its rules of behaviour."

Mergy looked at him with astonished eyes.

"Your brother is busy and cannot advise you; but if you will allow me I will endeavour to supply his place."

"I am ignorant, sir, what occasion——"

"You have been grievously insulted; and, seeing you in a thoughtful posture, I doubt not that you are musing on the means of vengeance."

" Vengeance! on whom?" said Mergy, blushing to the whites of his eyes.

" Did not little Comminges jostle you rudely just now? The whole Court saw the business, and expects you to take it seriously."

" But," said Mergy, " in so crowded a hall it is nothing wonderful that someone should have pushed me without intending it."

" M. de Mergy, I have not the honour to know you well, but your brother is my intimate friend, and he can tell you that I practise, as well as I can, the divine precept as to forgiving injuries. I should be very sorry to urge you into an unnecessary quarrel ; but at the same time I think it my duty to tell you that Comminges did not push you by accident. He pushed you because he wished to insult you ; and if he had not pushed you he would still have given you cause of offence ; for by picking up Madame de Turgis's glove he intruded upon a privilege which belonged to you. The glove was at your feet, therefore you only had the right to pick it up. Besides, you have only to turn your head, and you will see Comminges at the end of the gallery pointing the finger of scorn at you."

Mergy turned, and did perceive Comminges in the midst of a knot of young men telling some story to which they listened with interest. Nothing, it is true, showed that this group was talking of him ; but as his charitable adviser spoke Mergy felt his heart filled with violent rage.

" I will meet him after the hunt," said he, " and I will discover——"

" Never postpone a good resolution of this kind. Besides, it is much less of an offence to God to challenge your adversary immediately after the insult than to do it when you have had time for reflection. If you arrange a meeting in the heat of the moment, that is only a venial sin ; and if you fight afterwards, it is only to escape a much heavier crime, that of being false to your word. But I beg your pardon ; I had forgot that I speak to a

Protestant. Anyhow, arrang meeting ; I will bring him to of you at once."

" I trust he will not refuse me the a to which I am entitled."

"Do not deceive yourself, my good friend : Comminges has never pronounced the words 'I was wrong.' But all the same, he is a man of the nicest honour, and will give you every possible satisfaction."

Mergy did what he could to choke down all emotion and to assume a careless air.

"If I have been insulted," said he, "I must have satisfaction ; and whatever it is I shall know how to insist on it."

"'Tis well, my hero ; I am glad to see your pluck ; for you cannot be ignorant that Comminges is one of our best swordsmen. Faith ! 'tis a gentleman whose weapons are much at home in his hand. He learnt of Brambilla at Rome ; and Petit-Jean declines fencing with him any more."

And as he spoke he looked keenly at Mergy's face ; a face somewhat pale, but, as it seemed, rather with wrath at the insult than with fear at its consequences.

"I should like to be your second in the business ; but not to mention that to-morrow is my day for taking the sacrament, I am pledged to M. de Rheincy, and I cannot draw sword with anyone else." [1]

"I thank you, sir ; but if we come to extremities my brother will be my second."

"The captain is a very experienced gentleman in this kind of affair. Meanwhile I will bring Comminges to you for an explanation."

Mergy bowed, and turning towards the wall, he busied himself in arranging the terms of the challenge and in settling his countenance. There is a certain graceful manner of bidding defiance, which, like a good many other graceful habits, can only be learnt by practice. Now our hero was

[1] It was a point of honour for a *raffiné* not to enter into any new quarrel while he had one unsettled.

a beginner, and he therefore felt a little awkwardness ; but
for the moment he was much less afraid of receiving a sword-
thrust than of saying something unbecoming a gentleman.
He had, however, scarcely hit upon words at once resolute and polite, when the Baron de Vaudreuil, putting his
hand on his arm, sent them straight out of his head.

Comminges, hat in hand, and bowing with very insolent
politeness, said to him in a honeyed tone, " You wish to
speak to me, sir ? "

Mergy's face flushed with anger ; and he answered at
once, more firmly than he could have hoped, " You have
behaved to me in an insolent manner, and I demand satisfaction."

Vaudreuil nodded his head in approval ; but Comminges,
at once resuming an upright posture, and setting (as was
then proper in such cases) fist on hip, observed with much
gravity : " You present yourself then, sir, as challenger :
and I as challenged have the choice of arms."

" Take those which please you best."

Comminges appeared to reflect for a moment.

" The tuck," [1] he said, " is a good weapon, but it makes
ugly wounds ; and at our age," he added, smiling, " one
does not care to show a scar all over the face to one's
mistress. The rapier makes but a small hole, but 'twill
serve," and he smiled again. " Rapier and dagger, then,
for me."

" Very well," said Mergy; and he made as if he would
depart.

" One moment," said Vaudreuil ; " you have not agreed on
a meeting-place."

---

[1] *Estoc*, a large double-edged sword.

" All the Court goes to the Pré-aux-Cleres," said Comminges ; "and if, sir, you do not prefer another place——"

" The Pré-aux-Cleres be it."

" Then for the hour ? I shall not rise till eight o'clock, for private reasons which you will understand. Nor do I sleep at home to-night, and I could hardly be at the Pré before nine."

" At nine o'clock, then."

As Mergy turned his eyes away, he saw close to him the Countess de Turgis, who had left the captain in talk with another lady ; and it will be easily understood that at the sight of the fair causer of these harms, our hero charged his countenance with a double dose of solemnity and affected indifference.

" For some time past," said Vaudreuil, " the fashion has been to fight in scarlet drawers. If you have not got a pair ready made, I can lend you one. They make neater work : blood does not show on them."

" That seems to me childish," said Comminges ; and Mergy smiled a rather awkward assent.

" Well then, my friends," said the baron, who seemed quite in his element, " we have nothing more to do than to arrange the seconds and thirds for the meeting." [1]

" M. de Mergy," said Comminges, " is a newcomer at Court, and he might have some difficulty in finding a third. So I will be content with a second only, to oblige him."

Mergy, with some little difficulty, forced his lips into a sort of smile.

" Courtesy can go no farther," said the baron. " Indeed,

[1] The seconds were often not mere spectators, but fought themselves. The phrases " to second " " to third " someone were in use.

Q

it is a real pleasure to have to do with a gentleman so obliging as M. de Comminges."

" As you will need a rapier of the same length as mine," continued Comminges, " I recommend you Laurent, at the Golden Sun, in the Rue de la Ferronnerie. He is the best armourer in town. Tell him that I have sent you, and he will serve you well."

As he finished, he turned on his heel, and retired with much calmness to the knot of young men he had just left.

" I congratulate you, M. Bernard," said Vaudreuil ; " you managed your challenge excellently. 'Tis well—'tis very well ! Comminges is not accustomed to hear such language. He is feared like a pestilence, especially since he killed tall Canillac ; for as for St. Michel, whom he also killed two months ago, there was no great honour in that. St. Michel could not fence much ; while Canillac had already killed his man five or six times without a scratch. He had studied at Naples under Borelli ; and they said that Lansac on his deathbed had left him the secret of the pass with which he did so much mischief. To tell the truth, though," added he as if to himself, " Canillac had plundered the church of Auxerre and cast the host to earth, so there is no wonder that he was punished."

Mergy, who did not find these particulars amusing, felt nevertheless constrained to keep up the talk, for fear that some suspicion unfavourable to his gallantry should occur to Vaudreuil.

" Happily," said he, " I never plundered a church, and in my whole life have never even touched the host, so I have the less to fear."

" One counsel more, though. When you cross swords with Comminges, take special care of one of his tricks, which

cost Captain Tomaso his life. He cried out that his sword-
point was broken, and Tomaso raised his own sword above
his head, expecting a cut ; but Comminges's blade was
sound enough, for it went up to a foot from the hilt in
Tomaso's breast, which he had left unguarded, not expecting
the point. But as you are to use rapiers, there will be less
danger of this."

"I will do my best."

"Ah ! but listen. Mind you choose a dagger with a
stout shell ; it is invaluable for parrying. Do you see the
scar on my left hand ? I got that by going out without a
dagger one day. Young Tallard and I quarrelled, and I
was near losing my left hand for lack of a poniard."

"Was Tallard wounded ?" asked Mergy absently.

"I killed him, thanks to a vow which I made to Monseigneur Saint Maurice, my patron. But have some lint
and some linen about you ; 'twill do no harm, for a man is
not always killed out of hand. And it would be well to
have your sword put on the altar during mass-time. But
there, again, you are a Protestant. One word more : have
no punctilio about breaking ground, but give him as much
exercise as possible. He is not well-breathed ; pump him :
and when you get the chance, a good lunge in the chest,
and your man is done for."

He might have gone on a long time with this excellent
advice, if a loud flourish on the horns had not given warning
that the King was about to take horse. The door of the
Queen's apartments opened, and Their Majesties, in hunting
costume, made for the entrance steps.

Captain George, who had just left his lady, came to his
brother, and clapping him on the shoulder, said cheerfully:

"By the mass ! you are a lucky rascal ! Do you see

this young man with his kitten's whiskers? He no sooner shows himself than all the women are mad after him. Know you that your fair countess has been talking to me about you for a full quarter of an hour? Come, pluck up your spirits! Keep at her side during the hunt, and be as gallant as you can. But what the devil is the matter with you? You look ill, and your face is as long as a minister's at the stake. Be merry, man, confound you!"

"I do not care much about the hunt, and I should like——"

"If you do not hunt," whispered Vaudreuil, "Comminges will think you fear to meet him."

"Come along then," said Mergy, passing his hand over his heated brow, and reflecting that he had better wait till the hunt was over before telling his adventure to his brother. "'Twould be a shame," thought he, "if Madame de Turgis thought me afraid, or if she believed that the idea of a duel to come spoilt my pleasure in the sport."

CHAPTER X.

THE HUNT.

" The very butcher of a silk button,
a duellist, a duellist, a gentleman of
the very first house—of the first and
second cause : ah ! the immortal *pas-
sado!* the *punto reverso!*"—SHAKE-
SPEARE, *Romeo and Juliet.*

A GREAT number of
ladies and gentlemen,
richly dressed and splendidly
mounted, were passing in all
directions about the court of the
château. The blare of horns, the bay of the hounds, the
loud jests of the riders, made up a hubbub delightful to

the ears of a sportsman and hideous to those of every other human being.

Mergy mechanically followed his brother into the court-yard, and, hardly knowing what he did, found himself near the fair countess, already masked, and mounted on a fiery jennet, which pawed and champed the bit with impatience. But she, on a horse which would have tasked the full attention of an ordinary rider, seemed as much at her ease as though she were seated in an arm-chair at home. The captain made his way to her on the pretext of tightening the jennet's curb.

" Here is my brother," said he to the Amazon in a half-whisper, but loud enough for Mergy to catch his words. " Be kind to the poor boy; he has been hard hit ever since the day he saw you at the Louvre."

" I have forgotten his name already," she said, rather shortly ; " what is it ? "

" It is Bernard. Observe, madame, that his scarf is of the same colour as your ribbons."

" Can he ride ? "

" You shall see."

He bowed, and hastened off to the side of one of the Queen's ladies, to whom for some time past he had been paying his attentions ; and there, leaning over his saddlebow, with his hand on the fair one's bridle, he soon forgot all about his brother and his beautiful but haughty companion.

" You know Comminges then, M. de Mergy ? " asked Madame de Turgis.

" I, madame ? very little," answered he hesitatingly.

" Yet you were talking to him just now."

" It was for the first time."

" I think I guess what you said to him," replied she ; and

her eyes, through her mask, seemed to read to the bottom of Mergy's soul.

Here, to his great satisfaction, for the conversation embarrassed him alarmingly, a lady interrupted it by addressing the countess. But he continued to follow her, hardly knowing why; perhaps he thought it might annoy Comminges, who was watching him from a distance.

They left the château : a stag was started, and as he plunged into the forest all the hunt followed him. Mergy observed, not without surprise, the skill which Madame de Turgis showed in managing her horse, and the boldness with which she urged him across every obstacle in her way. He owed it only to the goodness of his own barb that he was not left behind ; but to his great annoyance the Count de Comminges, as well mounted as himself, also accompanied her, and despite the speed of a headlong gallop, despite his own special attention to the chase itself, frequently spoke to the fair horsewoman, while Mergy silently envied his light and careless deportment, and especially his skill in saying pleasant nothings which he thought must amuse the countess as much as they annoyed himself. As for other matters, the two rivals, urged by a noble emulation, found neither hedges high enough nor ditches wide enough to stop them, and risked both their necks twenty times over.

Suddenly the countess, leaving the main body of the hunt, struck into a ride diverging from that which the King and his following had entered.

"What are you doing ? " cried Comminges, " you are going wrong : do you not hear the horns and hounds on the other side ? "

" Well ; take the other ride if you like. Who prevents you ? "

Comminges made no answer, and followed her, as did Mergy. But when they had gone some hundreds of yards up the ride the countess slackened her pace, a movement which was imitated at once by Comminges to the right and Mergy to the left of her.

"That is a good charger of yours, M. de Mergy," said Comminges; "he has not turned a hair."

"'Tis a barb which my brother bought from a Spaniard. You may see the scar of a sword-wound he got at Montcontour."

"Have you served yourself?" said the countess to Mergy.

"No, madame."

"Then you have never received a shot-wound?"

"Never, madame."

"Nor a sword-thrust?"

"Nor that either."

Mergy thought he noticed a smile on her face. As for Comminges, he pulled his moustache with a sarcastic air.

"Nothing is more becoming to a young gentleman than a pretty wound," said he. "Do you not think so, madame?"

"Yes; if it is well won."

"What do you mean by well won?"

"I mean that a wound received on the battle-field is glorious. But it is different in a duel: I know nothing more despicable than that."

"I am to suppose that M. de Mergy had some conversation with you before getting to horse?"

"No," said the countess drily.

Mergy rode his horse close to Comminges. "Sir," whispered he, "as soon as we have rejoined the hunt we can turn into a thicket; and I shall hope to prove to you there that I have no desire of avoiding our meeting."

Comminges looked at him with a mixture of pity and approval.

"Good: I am very well disposed to believe you," answered he. "But as for your suggestion, I cannot accede to it. We are not nobodies to fight by ourselves; and our friends who are to be of the party would never forgive us for not waiting for them."

"As you like, sir," said Mergy, and he rode once more up to the side of Madame de Turgis, whose horse had made some paces in front. She rode with her head bowed on her breast, and seemed lost in thought; nor did the trio exchange a word till they reached an open space at the end of the ride into which they had struck.

"Is not that a bugle blast?" asked Comminges.

"I think it comes from the copse on our left," said Mergy.

"Yes, it is the horn; I am sure of it now; and a Bologna horn too. May I perish if it is not my friend Pompignan's. You would hardly believe, M. de Mergy, the difference between a true Bologna horn and those which our wretched Paris craftsmen make."

"That particular one certainly sends its sound far."

"And what a sound! How full! The very hounds as they hear it might forget that they have run ten leagues. In fact, nothing is really well made out of Italy and Flanders. What do you think of this Walloon ruff of mine? It suits a hunting dress well enough: I have ruffs and collars *à la confusion* to go to balls in; but this plain thing here, do you think they could make it in Paris? Not a whit: I got it from Breda. If you like, I can get you another from a friend of mine who is in Flanders. But——" and he broke off with a shout of laughter——"Begad! how thoughtless I am. I had quite forgotten——"

R

The countess drew bridle. " Comminges," she said, " the hunt is in front there, and to judge by the horn the stag is at bay."

" I think you are right, fair lady."

" And will you not be in at the death ?"

" Why, certainly ; otherwise our fame as huntsmen and horsemen is gone."

" Then you must make haste."

" Yes ; our horses have had time to breathe. Come, give us the word."

" For my part, I am tired, and shall stay here. M. de Mergy will bear me company. Now go."

" But——"

" Am I to tell you twice ? Set spurs to your horse."

But Comminges did not stir : his cheeks flushed, and he looked from Mergy to the countess with flaming eyes.

" Madame de Turgis desires a *tête-à-tête*," said he with a bitter smile

The countess pointed to the plantation whence came the sound of the horn, and with her finger-tips made a very significant motion of dismissal. But still Comminges seemed unable to make up his mind to leave the coast clear to his rival.

" It would seem that one may not mince matters with you. Be kind enough to leave us, M. de Comminges, for your company is troublesome. Do you understand me *now ?*"

" Entirely, madame," said he in a rage. And he added lower, " But as for this carpet-knight of yours, he will have no long time to amuse you in. Farewell, M. de Mergy ; we meet again." He laid a deep stress on the last words, and spurring hard, set off at a gallop.

The countess checked her own steed, which would have

followed the example, brought him to a walk, and for a time proceeded silently, raising her head now and then and looking at Mergy, as though she were about to speak, then turning her eyes away as if ashamed at being unable to find a phrase wherewith to begin.

It seemed to Mergy that the obligation of beginning rested with him.

"I am proud, madame, of the preference you have shown me," said he.

"Monsieur Bernard, can you fence?"

"Of course, madame," answered he with surprise.

"But can you fence well—very well, I mean?"

"Well enough for a gentleman, and badly, no doubt, for a fencing-master."

"But in our country gentlemen are too hard with the sword for professional masters."

"True. I have heard that many of our youth waste in fencing-rooms time they might better spend elsewhere."

" *Better?*"

" Why, yes. Is it not better worth while," said he smiling, " to talk with a lady than to perspire in a fencing-room ? "

" Tell me, have you been out often ?"

" Never once, madame, thank God ! But why all these questions ? "

" Learn, for your future instruction, that you should never ask a lady why she does this or that ; such at least is the custom of well-bred gentlemen."

" I am corrected, and will obey," said Mergy, smiling slightly, and bowing to his horse's mane.

" Then, what will you do to-morrow ?"

" To-morrow ?"

" Yes ; do not affect astonishment."

" Madame——"

" Answer me ; for I know all. Answer!" cried she, with a royal gesture of her hand towards him. Her finger-tip just touched Mergy's sleeve, and sent a shiver through him.

" I shall do my best," said he at last.

" I like the answer. 'Tis neither that of a coward nor that of a swaggerer. But you must know that you, a mere beginner, have to do with a very formidable enemy."

" What would you have ? I shall feel very awkward, no doubt, as I do now," added he smiling. " The only women I have seen have been peasant girls, and at my entrance on courtiership I find myself *tête-à-tête* with the fairest lady in the Court of France."

" Let us speak seriously. Comminges is the best swordsman of this Court, which is full enough of rufflers. He is the king of the *raffinés.*"

" So they say."

" Well, are you not anxious ? "

" I can only repeat that I shall do my best. One need never despair with a good sword, and, above all, with the help of God."

" The help of God!" said she scornfully. " Are you not a Huguenot, M. de Mergy?"

" I am, madame," said he with an air of gravity, as was his wont in reply to such a question.

" Then your risk is greater than another's."

" Why?"

" To endanger one's life is nothing; but you endanger more than your life—your soul."

" You speak, madame, according to the ideas of your own religion. Mine gives me more comfort."

" You are about to play a terrible losing game: eternity on one dice-throw, and sizes against you."

" But it would be the same, anyhow: for if to-morrow I died a Catholic, I should die in mortal sin."

" There is much to say on that head, and the difference is great!" cried she, vexed that Mergy should turn her own beliefs against her. " Our doctors will prove to you——"

" Oh, no doubt. They have proofs for everything. They take the liberty of changing the gospel itself to suit their fancies. For instance——"

" A truce with that! One cannot talk for a moment with a Huguenot but he brings in the Holy Scriptures on every subject."

" Because we read them; while your very priests know them not. But, as you say, let us change the subject. Do you think the stag is taken yet?"

" Then you are deeply attached to your religion?"

" It is you who are beginning again, madame."

" You think it a good one ? "

" Much more : I think it the best, the only good. I should change it else."

" But your brother has changed."

" He had his reasons for becoming a Catholic : I have mine for remaining a Protestant."

" They are all obstinate, and deaf to the voice of reason ! " cried she angrily.

" It will rain to-morrow," said Mergy, looking at the sky.

" M. de Mergy, my friendship for your brother and your own approaching danger make me feel an interest in you."

He bowed respectfully.

" You heretics, you believe not in relics ? "

He smiled.

" And you would think yourselves polluted by touching them ? " continued she. " You would refuse to wear them as we Roman Catholics are wont to do ? "

" The custom appears to us, to say the least, useless."

" Listen. One of my cousins once tied a relic to the neck of a hound, and then at twelve paces fired an arquebuss loaded with buck-shot at him."

" And the dog was killed ? "

" Not a shot touched him.

" That is really wonderful. I should like to have a relic like that."

" Indeed ? And you would wear it ? "

" Certainly. As the relic protected a dog, *a fortiori* —— But, wait a minute, is it sure that a heretic is worth a dog a Catholic's dog, of course ? "

Madame de Turgis paid no attention to him, but swiftly undid the buttons of her tight-fitting bodice, and drew from her bosom a little box of gold, quite flat in shape and fastened to a black ribbon.

"There!" said she; "you have promised to wear it; you must give it me back some day."

"If I can, I certainly will."

"But listen. You will take care of it? — no sacrilegious tricks! You will take the greatest care of it?"

"It comes from *you*, madame!"

She gave him the relic, which he took and put round his neck.

"A Catholic would have paid his thanks to the hand which gave him that holy talisman."

Mergy seized her hand, and tried to raise it to his lips.

"No, no; 'tis too late!"

"But think! I may never have such fortune again!"

"Take off my glove, then," said she, holding out the hand to him.

As he drew it off, he seemed to feel a slight squeeze, and he pressed a burning kiss on the white and lovely fingers.

"Monsieur Bernard," said the countess, in a voice full of emotion, "will you be headstrong to the end, and can nothing touch you? Will you at last be converted by my means?"

"I cannot tell," answered he, laughing. "But pray let your entreaties be strong and long. One thing is certain, no one shall convert me but you."

"Tell me frankly, if a woman — a woman who knew —— ."

She stopped.

"A woman who knew?"

"Yes. Is it possible that love —— But be candid! Speak to me seriously!"

"Seriously?" And he tried once more to seize her hand.

"Yes. Could the love which you might feel for a woman of another faith than yours—could not such a love make you change? God employs all sorts of means."

"And you would have me reply frankly and seriously?"

"I insist on it."

Mergy stooped his head, and was slow to reply. In fact, he was seeking for an evasive answer. He had no wish to repulse the advances which Madame de Turgis was making to him; but, on the other hand, a courtier of some hours' standing only, he still bore a country conscience terribly full of scruples.

"I hear the *hallali!*" cried the countess suddenly, without waiting for this answer which was so difficult to make. And touching her horse with her whip, she gallopped off, Mergy following her, but without receiving from her word or look. In a moment they had rejoined the hunt.

The stag had at first plunged into the midst of a pond, from which he was dislodged with difficulty by several riders, who dismounted, armed themselves with long poles, and obliged the poor beast to start afresh. But the cold of the water had completed the exhaustion of his strength. He left the pond,

panting, with tongue lolling out, and running in irregular
bounds. The hounds, on the other hand, seemed to redouble their eagerness ; but, at a short distance from the
pond, the stag, feeling that escape by flight was impossible,
seemed resolved to make a last effort, and, backing against
a massive oak, headed towards the hounds. The foremost
to attack were gored and tossed aloft, while a horse and
his rider were upset headlong. Warned by this, men, dogs,
and horses made a wide ring round the stag without daring
to come within reach of his threatening antlers.

The King dismounted lightly, and slipping, hunting-
knife in hand, adroitly behind the oak, houghed the stag
with a back stroke. The beast uttered a kind of hissing
groan, and fell at once. Immediately a score of hounds
dashed on him ; and, seized by throat, muzzle, and tongue,
he was pinned down, the large tears rolling from his eyes.

" Call the ladies closer !" cried the King ; and the ladies,
almost all of whom had dismounted, came near.

" Take that, *parpaillot !*" said he, plunging his hunting-
knife, which he turned in the wound to make it larger, into
the stag's side. The blood gushed forth with violence, and
covered the royal face and hands and dress. Now *parpaillot*
was a term of contempt which Catholics often applied to
Calvinists, and the word and the way in which it was used
offended many, while it was applauded by others.

" The King looks like a butcher," said young Téligny, the
Admiral's son-in-law, pretty loud, and with a disgusted air.
Nor did charitable souls, such as especially abound at Court,
fail to convey the observation to the monarch, who did
not forget it.

After enjoying the agreeable spectacle of the dogs devour-
ing the entrails of the deer, the Court returned to Paris.

On the way Mergy told his brother of the insult he had
received and the challenge which had followed. Advice
and remonstrance were in vain ; and the captain promised
to bear him company in the morning.

CHAPTER XI.

THE RAFFINÉ AND THE PRÉ-AUX-CLERCS.

"For one of us must yield his breath
Ere from the field one foot we flee."
The Duel of Stuart and Wharton.

NOTWITHSTANDING the fatigues of the chase, Mergy passed no small part of the night without sleeping. He turned feverishly from side to side in bed, and his fancy became abominably active under the excitement. A thousand thoughts, which had only an accidental connection or no connection at all with what was impending, beset and disturbed his brain; and more than once he

thought that the feverish disturbance he felt was but the pre-
lude of a serious illness which would show itself in a few
hours and confine him to bed. What would become of his
honour then? what would the world say? what, above all,
would Madame de Turgis and Comminges say? He would
have given much to hasten on the hour fixed for the
combat.

Luckily at sunrise he felt his blood course more steadily,
and he thought with less emotion of the coming meeting.
He dressed himself quietly, and even devoted some minute
attention to his toilette. He imagined the beautiful countess
hastening to the battle-field, finding him slightly wounded,
dressing the wound with her own hands, and making no
secret of her love. The stroke of eight on the clock of the
Louvre put these fancies to flight; and almost at the same
moment his brother entered the room. A deep sadness
marked his countenance, and it was pretty clear that he had
passed no better night; yet he forced a pleasant and cheerful
smile as he grasped Mergy's hand.

" Here," he said, "is a rapier for you, and a dagger with
shell-hilt, both by Luno of Toledo; see if the weight of
the sword suits you." And he threw on Mergy's bed a long
rapier and a poniard.

Mergy drew the sword, bent it, looked at the point, and
seemed satisfied. Then he directed his attention to the
poniard, the hilt of which was slashed with a vast number of
small holes, intended to catch the point of the adversary's
sword and hold it so that it could not be easily disengaged.

" With such good tools as these," said he, " I think I can
hold my own." Then, pointing to the relic which Madame
de Turgis had given him, and which he had kept hidden in
his bosom : " Here," he added, smiling, "is a talisman as

well, which preserves one from sword-thrusts better than any coat of mail."

" Where did you get that bauble ? "

" You may guess." And his pride in appearing as a ladies' darling made him for the moment forget both Comminges and the duelling sword which lay naked before him.

" I will bet that that mad countess has given it you. The devil take her and her box both."

" Don't you know that it is a charm which she has given me expressly for use to-day ? "

" She had better have shown herself gloved instead of seeking a chance of exhibiting her pretty white hand ! "

" God forbid," said Mergy, blushing deeply, " that I should believe in these Papist relics. But if I am to fall to-day I should like her to know that I fell with her gage on my breast."

" Coxcomb ! " cried the captain, shrugging his shoulders.

" Here is a letter for my mother," said Mergy, in a voice that trembled somewhat. George took it without a word, and, walking up to the table, opened a little Bible and read in it to settle his countenance, while his brother, completing his toilet, was busy in trussing the multitude of points which were then worn. On the first page that George opened he found these words in his mother's hand : " On the first of May, 1547, my son Bernard was born. Lord ! keep him in Thy ways. Lord ! preserve him from all evil." He bit his lips savagely, and threw the book on the table. Mergy, who saw the action, thought that some impious fancy had crossed his brother's brain ; he took up the Bible gravely, replaced it in its embroidered case, and locked it up in a cabinet with every mark of reverence. " 'Tis my mother's Bible," he said.

The captain answered not, but paced up and down the room.

"Ought we not to go?" said Mergy, buckling the belt of his sword.

"Not yet; we have plenty of time for breakfast."

Both took their places before a table covered with cakes of different kinds, which were flanked by a great silver tankard of wine. As they ate they argued at great length and with apparent interest on the merits of the liquor as compared with others in the captain's cellar, each attempting under cover of this trivial conversation to hide the real thoughts of his heart from his companion.

The captain rose first. "Let us go!" said he hoarsely; and crushing his hat over his eyes he hastily went downstairs.

They took boat and crossed the Seine, their boatman, who guessed by their appearance the errand which took them to the Pré-aux-Clercs, exhibiting great alacrity. As he pulled stoutly across he recounted to them with much circumstance how, the month before, two gentlemen, one of whom was called the Count de Comminges, had done him the honour to hire his boat in order to fight comfortably in it without fear of disturbance. M. de Comminges's adversary, whose name he was sorry not to have heard, had been run through the body and upset into the river as well; nor had he, the boatman, ever been able to fish him out.

As they touched land they saw a boat with passengers crossing the river some score of yards lower down. "There are our men," said the captain: "stay you here." And he ran to meet the boat, which carried Comminges and the Viscount de Béville.

"Ah!" cried the latter, "there you are! Is it you or

your brother that Comminges is going to kill?" And as he spoke he laughed and embraced him.

The captain and Comminges exchanged formal bows.

"Sir," said the captain to Comminges, as soon as he could disengage himself from Béville's embrace, "I think it my duty to make a last effort to prevent fatal consequences in a quarrel which is founded on no point of honour. I am sure that my friend will join his efforts to mine."

He pointed to Béville; but Béville grinned and shook his head.

"My brother," went on George, "is very young, and having no repute or experience in arms, he is obliged in consequence to show himself more punctilious than another might. Your reputation, sir, on the other hand, is made, and your honour can only gain by it if you will be good enough to admit, in my presence and M. de Béville's, that it was by oversight——"

Comminges interrupted him with a burst of laughter.

"Are you joking, my dear captain? or do you think me the sort of man to leave my lady's bower at this time and to cross the Seine in order to beg pardon of a schoolboy?"

"You forget, sir, that he of whom you speak is my brother; and you insult——"

"If he were your father, what does it matter to me? I care nothing for the whole family."

"Well then, sir, with your good leave, you shall have to do with the whole family; and as I am the eldest, you will please to begin with me."

"Pardon me, sir captain, I am bound by all the rules of the duello to fight with the person who challenged me first. Your brother's prior right is imprescriptible, as they say in the Palace of Justice. When I have finished with him I am at your commands."

"That is quite right," cried Béville; "and for my part I will consent to no other course of proceeding."

Mergy, astonished at the length of the colloquy, had approached slowly. He came up in time to hear his brother load Comminges with insults, even to the point of calling him coward, while Comminges replied with perfect coolness—

"After your brother's turn I will attend to you."

Mergy seized his brother's arm.

"George!" he cried, "is this the way you do me service? And would you wish me to take your part as you are trying to take mine? Sir," added he, turning to Comminges, "I am at your orders. We will begin as soon as you like."

"Then let us not lose a moment," said Comminges.

"Excellent, my dear fellow!" said Béville, grasping Mergy's hand. "You will go far, my boy, if we are lucky enough not to have to bury you here."

Comminges stripped off his doublet and undid the strings of his shoes, to signify that he would not retreat a step, as was the fashion with professional duellists. Mergy and Béville did the same; the captain alone had not so much as thrown off his cloak.

"What are you at, George, my friend?" said Béville. "Don't you know that you and I must have a turn together? We are none of the seconds who stand with folded arms while their friends fight. *We* follow the Spanish fashion."

The captain shrugged his shoulders.

"You think I am joking? I swear to you, by my

honour, that you must fight with me. The devil take me if you shall not!"

"You are a madcap and a fool," said the captain coolly.

"By Jove! you shall do me reason for those two little words, or you will drive me to take measures——" And he lifted his still sheathed sword, as though he would strike George.

"You will have it?" said the captain. "Be it so!" And in a second he had stripped to his shirt.

Comminges shook his sword in the air with a studied elegance, and at a single stroke made the scabbard fly twenty paces off. Béville tried to do the like, but the scabbard stuck half-way on the blade, which was held at the time to be at once a proof of awkwardness and a bad omen. The two brothers drew their swords with less flourish, but they too flung down the scabbards, which might have been in the way. Each man faced his foe, naked sword in the right hand, dagger in the left; and the four blades crossed at the same moment. First of all, George (by the device which Italian masters called then *Liscio di spada è cavare alla vita*,[1] and which consists in meeting the weak part of the sword with the strong, so as to deflect and beat down the adversary's blade) made Béville's sword fly from his hand, and set his own point at his antagonist's breast; but instead of running him through, he coolly lowered his weapon.

"You are no match for me," he said. "Do not wait till I am angry."

Béville had grown pale on seeing George's sword so close to his breast. A little out of countenance, he held

---

[1] To strike the blade and disengage at the body. All fencing terms were then borrowed from Italian.

T

out his hand to him; and both, sticking their swords in the ground, fixed their attention on the two principals.

Mergy was brave, and had plenty of coolness. He fenced well enough, and his bodily strength was much greater than that of Comminges, who seemed not to have recovered his exertions of the night before. For some time he confined himself to parrying with extreme care, breaking ground when Comminges pressed him too hard, and always keeping the point of his rapier at his adversary's face while he covered his own breast with the dagger.

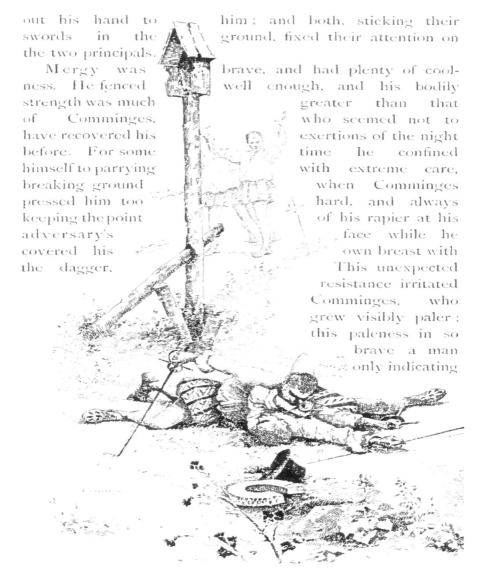

This unexpected resistance irritated Comminges, who grew visibly paler; this paleness in so brave a man only indicating excessive rage. His attacks grew faster and more furious, till in making a pass he beat up Mergy's sword with much skill, and, lunging fiercely, would certainly have run him through and through, save for an almost miraculous accident which spoilt the stroke. The point of the rapier struck the polished gold reliquary, which turned it and made it take an oblique direction; so that instead of penetrating Mergy's breast, the sword only pierced the skin, and, following a line parallel to the fifth rib, came out some two inches from the first incision. Before Comminges could draw back his sword, Mergy struck him with his dagger on the head so violently that he himself lost his balance and fell to the ground. Comminges dropped at the same time, so that the seconds thought them both dead.

Mergy was soon on his feet, and his first motion was to pick up his sword which he had let slip in his fall. Comminges did not stir. Béville lifted him up, and wiping with a handkerchief his face, which was drenched in blood, saw that the dagger had entered the eye, and that his friend had been killed on the spot, the steel having beyond all doubt pierced the brain.

Mergy stared at the corpse with haggard eyes.

" You are wounded, Bernard," said the captain, running up to him.

" Wounded!" cried Mergy; and then only did he notice that his shirt was bloody.

" 'Tis nothing," said the captain; " the blow slipped." He stanched the blood with his handkerchief, and asked for Béville's to complete the dressing. Béville let the body which he held fall back on the sward, and at once gave, not only his own handkerchief, but that of Comminges, which he fetched from his doublet.

"Zooks! friend," cried he, "what a dagger-stroke! You have something like an arm! Death of my life! what will our gentlemen *raffinés* of Paris say if the provinces send up gallants of your kidney? Pray you, tell me, how many duels have you fought already?"

"Alas!" said Mergy, "this is the first. But in God's name look to your friend."

"He wants no looking to, by Jove! after the way you have handled him. The dagger has pierced the brain, and the blow was dealt so featly and hard that—look at his cheek and eyebrow! The shell of the poniard has stamped itself on them like a seal on wax."

Mergy shivered all over, and great tears began to trickle down his cheeks.

Béville picked up the dagger and looked curiously at the flutings full of blood. "Here is a tool," said he, "to which Comminges's younger brother ought to burn a stout candle. This pretty poniard estates him in a splendid fortune."

"Let us go; take me hence," said Mergy in a stifled voice, seizing his brother's arm.

"Do not distress yourself," said George, as he helped him to put on his doublet. "After all, the man you have killed is not particularly worth mourning."

"Poor Comminges!" cried Béville; "to think that you, who have fought a hundred times, were killed by a young-ster in his first duel! Poor Comminges!" And this was the end of his funeral sermon.

But as he cast a last look on his friend Béville perceived the defunct's watch hanging, as was then the fashion, from his neck. "By Jove!" cried he, "you have no need to know the time of day now." And he undid and pocketed the watch, remarking that Comminges's brother would be quite rich enough as it was, and that he himself should like a keepsake of his friend.

As the two brothers were moving off, "Wait for me," he cried out to them, putting on his doublet hastily. "Ah, Monsieur de Mergy, you are forgetting your dagger. Do not lose that, at any rate," and he wiped the blade on the dead man's shirt and ran to catch up the young duellist. "Console yourself, my dear fellow," he said, as he slipped into his boat. "Do not pull such a rueful countenance. Take my advice, and instead of bemoaning yourself, pay a visit this very day fresh from this business to your mistress, and try if you cannot give a citizen to the State in the place of him of whom you have deprived it. Then will the world have lost nothing by you. Come, boatman, pull as if you wished to earn a pistole. There are some gentry with halberds coming towards us; they must be the watch from the Tour de Nesle, and we do not want to have anything to do with them."

CHAPTER XII.

WHITE MAGIC.

"Last night I dreamt of dead fish and broken eggs; and I have learnt from Master Anaxarchus that broken eggs and dead fish betoken ill-luck."—MOLIÈRE, *Les Amants Magnifiques.*

THE halberdiers were in fact some of the soldiers of the watch, a troop of whom was always stationed in the neighbourhood of the Pré-aux-Clercs, so as to be ready to interpose in the quarrels which were wont to be settled on this ground sacred to duels. According to their custom, they had come up very slowly, and so as not to reach the spot till all was over. For, to tell the truth, their peacemaking intentions were often very ill received; and more than once desperate enemies had been known to suspend a mortal combat in order to attack, side by side, the soldiers who tried to part them. Thus the functions of the guard were usually limited to helping the wounded or carrying off the dead. In this instance the archers had but the latter duty to accomplish, and they did it according to their custom, that is to say, after very carefully emptying the pockets and dividing the garments of the unlucky Comminges.

" My advice to you, my dear friend," said Béville, turning to Mergy, " is to have yourself taken as quietly as possible to Master Ambrose Paré, who is a precious man for sewing you up a wound or putting a broken limb to rights. Though he is as rank a heretic as Calvin himself, he is in such repute that the hottest Catholics resort to him. Up to this time nobody but the Marchioness de Boissières has faced death bravely rather than owe life to a Huguenot, for which reason I will wager ten pistoles that she is in Paradise."

" The wound is nothing," said George; " it will be healed in three days. But Comminges has relations at Paris, and I fear they may take his death a little too seriously."

" Ah, yes; there is a mother, who will think herself obliged by decency to prosecute our friend. But there! get M. de Châtillon to beg his pardon, and the King will grant it at once. He is as wax in the Admiral's hands."

" If it may be so," said Mergy in a feeble voice, " I should prefer that the Admiral knew nothing at all about the matter."

" Why? do you think the old greybeard will be vexed to hear what short work a Protestant has made of a Catholic?"

But Mergy only answered by a deep sigh.

"Comminges was too well known at Court for his death not to make some noise," said the captain. "But you did your duty like a gentleman, and nothing but honour can redound to you from the whole thing. It is long since I paid old Châtillon a visit, and this will be an opportunity of renewing our acquaintance."

"As it is never pleasant to find oneself clapped under the law's bolts and bars, even for an hour or two," continued Béville, "I will bestow your brother in a house where they will not think of looking for him. He can be quite quiet there till his business is settled; for as a heretic they could perhaps hardly give him sanctuary in a convent."

"Thanks for your offer, sir," said Mergy: "but I cannot accept it, for I might compromise you by doing so."

"Not a whit, not a whit, my dear fellow; and if you did, a man must stand by his friends. The house where I mean to lodge you belongs to a cousin of mine who is away from Paris for the time, and it is mine to do what I like with. Indeed, there is someone there already to whom I have given a lodging, and who will look after you: an old lady who is very obliging to us youth, and is devoted to me. She knows leechcraft, magic, astronomy, heaven knows what; and her most convenient talent of all is that of go-between. Blast me, but she would take a love-letter to the Queen herself if I asked her!"

"Well, then," said the captain, "we will take him there as soon as Master Ambrose has given him the first dressing." They touched the right bank as he spoke, and after hoisting Mergy with some trouble on a horse, they took him to the famous surgeon, and thence to a lonely house in the Faubourg Saint Antoine. Nor did they leave him till night saw him tucked up in a comfortable bed, and specially recommended to the old woman's care.

When you have killed a man, and when this man is the first that you have killed, you are haunted for some time, and especially at nightfall, by the memory and the look of the last struggle that ushered in his death. The mind is so full of gloomy thoughts, that it is hard to take part even in the most trivial conversation; all talk wearies and annoys; while, on the other hand, solitude is dreaded because it strengthens the oppression of fancy. Despite the frequent visits of Béville and the captain, Mergy spent the days immediately succeeding his duel in the deepest sadness. A sharp touch of fever, brought on by his wound, kept him sleepless at night, and this was his worst time. Only the notion that Madame de Turgis thought of him and had admired his courage consoled him a little, but did not restore him to calm.

One night, oppressed by the stifling heat (for it was the month of July), he took a fancy to leave his room, in order to walk and breathe the air in a garden, full of trees, which surrounded the house. He threw a cloak over his shoulders, and was about to go forth, when he found that his chamber door was locked on the outside. It could only be, he thought, a slip of his old nurse, and as she slept at a distance, and must probably be fast asleep, he thought it quite useless to call her; besides, his window was near the ground, which was soft below, having been recently dug. In a moment he had dropped into the garden. The night was dark; not a star blinked; and scanty puffs of wind now and then, and as though with difficulty, crossed the hot and heavy atmosphere. It was about two o'clock in the morning, and profound stillness reigned around him.

Mergy paced for some time, absorbed in thoughts, which were
interrupted by a knock at the street
gate. It was a faint, and, as it were,
mysterious stroke of the knocker,
whosoever struck it seeming assured that someone would be ready
to open. A visitor at a lonely
house and at such an hour was
something surprising, and Mergy
kept himself motionless in a dark
corner of the garden, whence he
could see everything without being
seen. A woman, who could not
be other than his old nurse, came
out of the house at once
with a dark lantern in her
hand : she opened the gate,
and there entered someone
wrapped completely in a large
black hooded mantle.

Bernard's curiosity was in
a state of lively excitement.
The stature, and, so far as he
could judge, the garments, of
the newcomer indicated the
other sex; and the old woman
greeted her visitor with every mark
of respect, while Blackmantle
scarcely bowed her head in return.
To make amends she put something into the old woman's hand,

which seemed to be received with pleasure, while the sharp
sound as of metal dropping, and the eagerness with which
the hag stooped and looked about on the ground, convinced
Mergy that she had had money given to her.   The two
women then walked towards the garden, the crone going first
and hiding her lantern.   At the garden's end there was a
kind of arbour formed by limes, which were planted in a
circle, and joined together by a very thick hedge nearly as
close as a wall.   Two gates or entries led into this green
retreat, in the centre of which was a small stone table.
Into this the old woman and the veiled visitor entered.
Mergy, holding his breath, and following them with stealthy
step, placed himself behind the hedge, so that he could hear
perfectly, and could see as well as the scanty light illumi-
nating the scene permitted.

The old woman began by lighting something, which burnt
up at once, in a tripod placed on the middle of the table,
and gave a pale bluish light, like that of salt and spirits of
wine mingled together.   She forthwith extinguished or
covered up her lantern, so that by the flickering light of
the tripod Mergy would have had difficulty in recognizing
the stranger's features, even if they had not been hidden by
veil and hood.   As for the old woman, it was easy to recognize her stature and figure; but he noticed that her face
was smeared with some dark dye which made her, under
her white coif, look like a bronze statue.   The table was
covered with singular objects which he could hardly dis-
tinguish.   They seemed arranged in regular though eccentric
order; and he thought he saw amongst them fruit, pieces
of bone, and some fragments of blood-stained linen.   Above
these soiled rags stood a little figure of a man, of wax, as it
seemed, and at most a foot high.

"Well, Camilla," said the veiled lady in a low voice, which made Mergy start, "you say he is better?"

"A little better, madame," said the hag, "thanks to our art. Still, with these scraps and the little blood there is on the bandages, it has been difficult for me to do much."

"And what says Master Ambrose Paré?"

"He, the dunce! What does it matter what he says? I give you my word that the wound is deep, dangerous, and terrible, and that it can only be cured by the rules of magic sympathy. But it is needful to do frequent sacrifice to the spirits of earth and air; and for sacrifice——"

The lady understood her at once.

"If he is cured," she said, "you shall have double what I have just given you."

"Be of good hope, and rely on me."

"Ah, Camilla! but if he should die?"

"Calm yourself. The spirits are favourable; the stars protect us; and our last sacrifice of the black ram has propitiated The *Other*."

"I bring you something that has cost me much pains to procure. I bought it of one of the archers who stripped the corpse."

She drew an object from beneath her cloak, and Mergy caught the glitter of a sword-blade. The hag took it, and held it close to the light for examination.

"Thank heaven! there is blood and rust on the blade! Yes! his blood is as that of the basilisk of Cathay—it leaves an ineradicable trace on the steel."

She looked carefully at the blade; and it was clear that the veiled lady felt more than ordinary emotion.

"See, Camilla! how near the blood is to the hilt. The blow may be mortal."

" That blood is not heart's blood : he will recover."

" He will recover ? "

" Yes ; but he will pay for his recovery by catching an incurable disease."

" What disease ? "

" Love."

" Ah, Camilla ! are you speaking the truth ? "

" When did I ever fail to speak the truth ?   When did my predictions fail in accomplishment ?   Did I not tell you that he would be victorious in the fight ?   Did I not inform you that the spirits would fight on his side ?   Did I not bury, on the very spot where the duel was to take place, a black hen and a sword blessed by the priest ? "

" It is true."

" Did you not yourself drive a dagger into the heart of an image of his adversary, thus directing the blows of him in whose behalf I spent my skill ? "

" Yes, Camilla, I did pierce the heart of Comminges's image.   But they say that he died of a wound in the head."

" Of course, the steel struck his head ; but did he not die because the blood stopped at his heart ? "

The veiled lady seemed crushed by the weight of this argument, and she was silent. Meanwhile the hag moistened the sword-blade with oil and balsam, and wrapped it with the greatest care in bandages.

" See, madame," she said, " this scorpion's oil with which I rub the sword is directed by virtue of sympathy into the young man's wound.   He feels the effect of this African balsam just as if I poured it on his hurt ; and if I took a fancy to let the sword-point grow red hot in the fire, our poor patient would suffer as much as though he were burnt alive."

" Oh! think not of such a thing."

" One evening I sat by the hearth busily rubbing a sword with balsam to cure a young gentleman in whose head that sword had made two fearful wounds. I fell asleep at my task, when suddenly the sick man's lackey knocked at my door to tell me that his master was suffering the

agonies of death, and that when he had left him he felt as if stretched on blazing coals. Do you know what had happened? I had carelessly let the sword slip, and the blade was at the moment on the embers. I snatched it off, and told the lackey that he would at his return find his master fully relieved. I plunged the sword at once in iced water, with a mixture of certain drugs, and went to see my patient. As I entered he cried to me, 'Ah! my good Camilla, what sweet relief I feel now! It seems as though I were in a bath of cool water, while just now I might have been St. Laurence on his gridiron.'"

She finished dressing the sword, and said with a satisfied air, "'Tis well: now I am sure of his cure, and you may give your attention to the last ceremony." She threw some pinches of sweet-smelling powder on the flame, and muttered outlandish words, crossing herself continually. Then the lady took the waxen image with a trembling hand, and holding it above the tripod she pronounced these words in a voice full of passion : "*As this wax softens and burns in the tripod flame; so, O Bernard Mergy! may thy heart grow soft and burn for love of me!*"

"Good : now here is a green wax candle moulded at midnight in accordance with the rules of art. Light it to-morrow before the Virgin's altar."

" I will ; but in spite of all your promises I am terribly anxious. I dreamt yesterday that he was dead."

" Were you sleeping on your right side or your left ? "

" On ——but which side do true dreams come ? "

" Tell me first on which side you sleep. I see that you wish to abuse and deceive yourself."

" I always sleep on my right side."

" Then be composed. Your dream announces nothing but good luck."

"God grant it ! But I saw him pale, bleeding, and wrapped in his shroud——"

As she spoke, she turned her head and saw Mergy standing at one of the arbour doors. Her astonishment made her shriek so piercingly, that Mergy himself was confounded. The hag, either purposely or by accident, upset the tripod, and at once there rose to the summit of the limes a flash of brilliant light that blinded him for a moment or two, during which the two women escaped, without losing an instant, through the opposite entrance. As soon as Mergy could discern the opening in the hedge he tried to follow them ; but at his first movement he scarcely saved himself from a fall, something having got between his legs. This he recognized as the sword to which he owed his cure. He lost some further time in getting clear of it and exploring the way, and when, reaching a wide straight alley, he thought that there could be no more obstacles to his catching the fugitives, he heard the street gate shut. They were out of reach.

A little vexed at having let so fair a prey slip through his fingers, he groped his way back to his chamber, and threw himself on the bed. All doleful thoughts were banished from his mind, and both remorse, if he had had any, and the anxiety which his condition had caused him, disappeared as if by enchantment. He thought of nothing but the happiness of loving and being loved by the most beautiful woman in Paris : for he could not doubt that the veiled lady was Madame de Turgis. A little after sunrise he fell asleep ; and only woke when it had been broad day for several hours. Upon his pillow he found a sealed billet which had been placed there, he knew not how ; and opening it, he read these words : " Sir knight, a lady's honour depends on your discretion."

A few moments afterwards the old woman came in to

X

bring him some broth. She wore for the day, contrary to
her custom, a rosary of large beads, hung to her girdle.
Her skin, carefully washed, showed no longer like bronze,
but like smoked parchment, and she walked with slow steps
and downcast eyes, like a person who fears to be troubled in
her commerce with the skies by the sight of earthly things.

Mergy thought that, for the more deserving practice of
the virtue recommended to him in the mysterious note, he
had better first acquire a thorough knowledge as to what he
was to keep secret from the world. So holding the broth in
his hand, and giving old Martha no time to reach the door,
he said, " You never told me that your name was Camilla ? "

" Camilla ? My name is Martha, good gentleman—Martha
Micheli," said the old woman, affecting great surprise at his
question.

" Very well ; so be it. You are to be called Martha by
men ; but spirits know you under the name of Camilla."

" Spirits ? Sweet Jesus ! What do you mean ? " and she
crossed herself all over.

" Come ; no tricks with me. I will tell no one, and all
this is between ourselves. Who is the lady who takes such
interest in my health ? "

" The lady who—— ? "

" Now, do not repeat my words, but speak frankly. On
the faith of a gentleman I will not betray you."

" Truly, good gentleman, I know not what you would
say."

Mergy could not help a laugh as he saw her feign astonishment, and lay her hand on her heart. He took a piece of
gold from the purse that hung at his bed-head and offered
it to the old woman.

" Come, good Camilla, you take so much care of me, and

give yourself so much trouble in rubbing swords with scorpion's balm, all for the sake of curing me, that really I ought to have made you a present long ago."

"Alas! gentleman, indeed, indeed, I understand no word of what you say."

"Confusion! Martha, or Camilla if you like, don't make me angry, but answer. Who is the lady for whom you performed all that pretty witchcraft last night?"

"Oh! gracious Saviour! he is getting angry! Can he be delirious?"

Mergy, in a rage, seized his pillow and flung it at her head. The old lady replaced it with much humility on the bed, picked up the gold crown from the floor where it had fallen, and, as the captain entered at the same moment, she was relieved of her fear of a cross-examination, which might have ended awkwardly for her.

CHAPTER XIII.

SLANDER.

"King Henry IV. Thou dost belie him, Percy ; thou dost belie him."
SHAKESPEARE, *King Henry IV.*

GEORGE had gone to see the Admiral that same morning, in order to inform him of his brother's misadventure, and had told the whole story in a few words.

The Admiral, as he listened, crunched the toothpick which he had in his mouth—a sure sign of ill-temper with him.

"I knew this matter already," said he; "and I am surprised that you should speak of it, for it is notorious enough."

" If I trouble you, my Lord Admiral, it is but because I know the interest you condescend to take in our family, and I venture to hope that you will graciously solicit the King's clemency to my brother. Your credit with his Majesty——"

" My credit, if I have any," broke in the Admiral sharply, " my credit depends upon the fact that I never put any but just demands before his Majesty." And as he spoke the last word he lifted his hat reverentially.

" The circumstance which makes it necessary for my brother to have recourse to your goodness is unfortunately one but too common in these days. Last year the King signed more than fifteen hundred writs of pardon, and Bernard's adversary himself has repeatedly enjoyed the protection which these writs give."

" Your brother was the aggressor ; though, perhaps, and I would it were true " (he looked steadily at George as he spoke), " he has but followed pernicious advice."

" I did my best to prevent the fatal results of this quarrel ; but you know that M. de Comminges was of a temper to give no satisfaction to anyone but at point of sword. The honour of a gentleman and the opinion of ladies——"

" Then that is how you talk to the young man ? " said the Admiral. " Perhaps you hope to make a *raffiné* of him ? How would his father mourn if he knew in what manner his son despises his counsel! Good God! 'tis but two years since our civil wars were quenched, and men have already forgotten the oceans of blood shed in them. Their thirst is not yet slaked. Every day some Frenchmen must cut other Frenchmen's throats."

" If I had known, sir, that my petition was likely to displease you———"

" Listen to me, M. de Mergy. I might, perhaps, do violence to my sentiments as a Christian, and excuse your brother's action in giving the challenge. But according to public report his conduct in the duel which followed was not——"

" What mean you, Admiral ?"

" That the fight was not conducted in a loyal manner and according to the custom of French gentlemen."

" Who has dared to spread so infamous a slander ?" cried George, his eyes flashing with rage.

" Be calm. You can send no challenge on this score, for as yet we do not fight with women. Comminges's mother has given the King details which do not reflect credit on your brother, and which may, perhaps, explain how so redoubtable a swordsman succumbed thus easily to the blows of a boy scarcely out of pagehood."

" A mother's sorrow is deep and sacred," said George. " Is it surprising that she cannot see the truth through eyes still bathed in tears ? I cannot but hope, sir, that you will abstain from condemning my brother on the faith of Madame de Comminges's story."

Coligny seemed moved, and his voice lost something of its sharply ironical tone.

" Yet you cannot deny that Béville, Comminges's second, is your own intimate friend ?"

" I have indeed known him long, and owe him something. But Comminges was as intimate with him as I, and Comminges himself chose him for his second. Besides, Béville's gallantry and honour put him above all suspicion of disloyal conduct."

The Admiral pursed his mouth in deep disdain.

" The honour of Béville !" he repeated, shrugging his

shoulders. "The honour of an Atheist! of a man
steeped in debauchery!"

"Yes!" cried the captain, laying stress on
his words, "Béville *is* a man of honour. But
why all this talk? Was I not myself
present at this duel? Is it for you,

Sir Admiral, to question the
honour of our house and
accuse us of assassination?"

There was a touch of menace in his
tone; but Coligny either did not understand, or despised, the allusion to the murder
of Duke Francis of Guise, which Catholics in their hatred
had attributed to himself. His features even relapsed into
unruffled calm.

"M. de Mergy," said he in a cold and contemptuous tone, "a man who has denied his faith has lost the right to talk of his honour, for none would believe in it."

The captain's face first flushed purple, and then turned deadly pale. He fell back a step, as though to avoid the temptation of striking the old man.

"Sir!" he cried, "your age and your rank allow you to insult with impunity the most precious possession of a poor gentleman. But I beg of you to bid one of your followers, or more than one, to endorse the words which you have spoken. I swear, by God, that they shall swallow those words till they choke."

"That may be a practice with the gentry called *raffinés*. I follow not their manners, and I discard those of my gentlemen who imitate them."

And he turned his back on George as he spoke. The captain, with fury in his heart, left the Hotel de Châtillon, sprang on his horse, and, as if to relieve his wrath, made the poor animal gallop at full speed by digging his spurs into his sides. In his headlong career he just escaped riding down no small number of peaceable passers-by; and it may be considered lucky that not a single specimen of the *raffinés* themselves met him, for in the temper in which he was he would certainly have lost no occasion of drawing sword.

When he had got as far as Vincennes his heated blood began to cool. He turned bridle, and brought his horse, drenched in sweat and blood, back towards Paris. "Poor friend!" said he, smiling bitterly, "I am punishing you for his insult to myself." And patting the innocent victim's neck, he rode slowly back to his brother's house, where, omitting all the details of the conversation, he simply told Mergy that the Admiral refused to interfere.

Y

But a few minutes afterwards Béville came in, and, throwing himself forthwith on Mergy's neck, said, "Congratulations, my dear fellow! Here is your pardon, which you owe to the Queen's intercession."

Mergy was less surprised than his brother, and in his heart of hearts he ascribed this favour to the veiled lady, that is to say, to Madame de Turgis.

CHAPTER XIV.

THE ASSIGNATION.

"Madame to this saloon will shortly walk,
And begs the favour of a moment's talk."
MOLIÈRE, *Tartufe*.

MERGY resumed his share of his brother's apartments ; he paid a visit of thanks to the Queen-Mother, and reappeared at Court. But he had scarcely set foot in the Louvre when he perceived that he had in some sort fallen heir to the consideration which Comminges had enjoyed. People whom he only knew by sight bowed to

him with an air of humble attempt at intimacy ; men, as they
spoke to him, hid their envy but ill under a markedly polite
outside, and the ladies' eyes rained provocations upon him, for
at that time to obtain the reputation of a successful duellist
was the surest road to their hearts.   To have killed three
or four men in single combat supplied the want of good
looks, of wealth, and of wit.   In short, as our hero showed
himself in the gallery of the Louvre, he heard whispered
remarks all round him.   " There is young Mergy, who killed
Comminges !"   " How young he is !"   " What a good figure !"
" What an air !"   " What a well-curled moustache !"   " Is it
known who his mistress is ?"

But Mergy looked in vain through the crowd for the blue
eyes and black eyebrows of Madame de Turgis.   He even
made a visit at her house ; but he learnt that shortly after
Comminges's death she had left for one of her estates, which
was some twenty leagues from Paris.   If ill tongues were
to be believed, her sorrow at the death of her lover had
forced her to seek a retreat where she might nurse her grief
undisturbed.

One morning, while the captain, stretched on a sofa, was
reading as he waited for breakfast " The Very Horrific Life
of Pantagruel," and while his brother was taking a lesson on
the guitar from Signor Uberto Vinibella, a lackey came to
tell Bernard that an old woman, very decently dressed, was
waiting for him in the lower hall, and that she had asked for
an interview with an air of mystery.   He went down at
once, and received from the sunburnt hands of a dame
who was neither Martha nor Camilla, a letter breathing
sweet perfumes.   It was fastened with a golden thread and
a large seal of green wax, whereon, instead of arms, nothing
was seen but a cupid with finger on lip, and the Spanish

motto " CALLAD."[1]   He opened it, and found only one line in the same language, which he construed with some difficulty : " *Esta noche, una dama espera à V. M.*"[2]

" Who gave you this letter ?" said he to the old woman.

" A lady."

" Her name ?"

" I know not ; she says she is a Spaniard."

" How does she know me ?"

The crone shrugged her shoulders. " Your reputation for gallantry has brought this ugly affair on you," she said sarcastically. " But answer me, will you come ?"

" Where am I to go ?"

" Be this evening, at half-past eight o'clock, in the church of St. Germain l'Auxerrois, towards the left side of the nave."

" And shall I see this lady at church ?"

" No ; someone will be there to conduct you to her. But be discreet, and come alone."

" Of course."

" You promise ?"

" I pledge you my word."

" Farewell, then ; and follow me not."

She curtseyed low, and departed.

" Well, what did my lady go-between want with you ?" asked the captain, when his brother had gone upstairs and the music-master had taken his leave.

" Oh, nothing," said Mergy carelessly, and examining attentively the Madonna of which mention has been made.

" Come, no secrets with me. Must I escort you to an assignation ? Shall I mount guard in the street, and keep off rivals with the flat of my sword ?"

[1] " Be silent."
[2] " A lady expects you this evening."

" Nothing of the kind, I tell you."

" Oh, just as you like. Keep your counsel if you please ; but I will bet that you are at least as much dying to tell as I am to know."

Mergy, with an absent air, twitched the strings of his guitar.

" By the way, George," said he, " I shall not be able to go and sup to-night with M. de Vaudreuil."

" Oho! it is for to-night, then ? Is she pretty ? Is she a Court lady, or a citizen's wife, or a trader's ?"

" Really I do not know. I am to be introduced to a lady who is not of this country ; but who it is I know not."

" But you know at least where the meeting-place is ?"

Bernard showed him the note, and repeated what the crone had said.

" It is a feigned hand," said the captain ; "and I do not know what to think of all these precautions."

" She must be some great lady, George."

" How like these youngsters that is! To fancy, on the least excuse, that queens and princesses are going to fling themselves at their heads !"

" But smell the perfume which the letter breathes."

" What on earth does that prove ? "

The captain's brow suddenly darkened as a sinister thought occurred to his mind.

" The Comminges are not a forgiving family," said he ; "and this letter may be only a trick of theirs to decoy you into some out-of-the-way corner, where they will make you pay dear for the dagger-thrust which gave them their inheritance."

" A pretty notion !"

" It would not be the first time that Love has been made

to do Revenge's work. You have read your Bible : remember Samson and the traitress Delilah."

" I should be a coward indeed if such an improbable guess made me baulk a meeting which may be so charming. A Spanish lady !"

" At any rate, go well armed. If you like, you can have the two lackeys."

" Fie on you ! What ! call the whole town to witness my good fortune ? "

" It is quite usual now," said George. " I have often seen my good friend D'Ardelay setting out to visit his lady-love with a mail shirt on his back, a pair of pistols in his belt, and four soldiers of his company marching behind him, each man with a loaded petronel. You don't know Paris yet, my friend ; and you may take my word for it, too much forethought never does harm. You have nothing to do but to take your mail shirt off when it is in the way."

" I do not feel the least anxiety. If Comminges's relations had a grudge against me, they could have attacked me any night in the streets."

" Well, then, I will let you go ; but only on condition that you take your pistols."

" As you like ; but I shall be laughed at for doing it."

" Nor is that all. You must make a good dinner, and eat two partridges and plenty of cock's-comb pasty, that you may do credit to the race of Mergy to-night."

Bernard retired to his room, where he spent at least four hours in combing and curling his hair, in perfuming himself, and finally in arranging eloquent discourse intended for the benefit of the fair unknown.

I may leave my readers to guess whether he was punctual at the meeting-place or not. He had paced the

church for full half an hour, and had
already thrice counted the candles, the
pillars, and the votive offerings, when
an old woman, carefully enveloped in
a brown cloak, took his hand, and, without
speaking a word, led him into
the street. She conducted him,
still in perfect silence, by
several twists and turns into
a very narrow and apparently
uninhabited alley. At the
very end of it, she stopped

in front of a door—small, arched, and very low—which she opened with a key drawn from her pocket. She led the way in, and Mergy followed, holding her cloak to guide himself through the darkness. Nor had he sooner entered than he heard huge bolts drawn behind him. His guide then warned him in a whisper that he was at the foot of a staircase, and that there were twenty-seven steps to mount. The stair was very narrow, and the worn and irregular steps more than once nearly brought him down; but at length, after the twenty-seventh step and a small landing were passed, the old woman opened a door from which a flood of light dazzled Mergy's eyes for the moment. Then he set foot in an apartment much more elegantly furnished than the external appearance of the house promised.

The walls were covered with flowered tapestry, a little faded, perhaps, but still in perfectly good condition. In the midst of the room he saw a table, lighted with two candles of rose-coloured wax, and covered with various kinds of fruit and cakes, together with glasses and flasks of crystal ; the latter filled, as it seemed, with different kinds of wine. Two large chairs, placed at the two ends of the table, waited apparently for the guests. In a recess, half closed by silken curtains, was a bed of very ornate design, covered with crimson satin, while more than one incense-burner shed a voluptuous perfume over the apartment.

The crone took off her mantle ; and Mergy, doffing his cloak, at once recognized the messenger who had brought him the letter.

" Saint Mary !" cried she, as she saw his sword and pistols, " do you think you have got to hew down giants ? there are no sword-blows, fair knight, to deal here."

" I hope so ; but it may be that some brothers or an ill-tempered husband may disturb the meeting ; and in that case here is something to keep them quiet with."

" You need fear nothing of that kind here. But tell me, how do you like the room ? "

" It is a fair chamber, doubtless ; yet should I grow weary of it if I had to stay here alone."

" You shall have company anon. But meanwhile you must promise me something."

" What ? "

" If you are a Catholic, you must lay your hand on this crucifix," and she took one from a cupboard : " if you are a

Huguenot, you must swear by Luther, by Calvin, by all your gods—in short   "

" But what must I swear ? " said he smiling.

" You must swear to make no attempt to find out who is the lady who is coming here."

" 'Tis a hard condition."

" See, now : you must swear, or I shall take you back into the street."

" There, then ; you have my word for it, and that is as good as the foolish oaths you propose."

" 'Tis well. Now wait patiently ; eat and drink, if you care to do so ; and without delay you shall see the Spanish lady come."

She took her mantle and went out, double-locking the door.

Mergy threw himself into a chair. His heart beat violently ; and he felt an emotion as strong as that which he had experienced a few days before, when about to meet his enemy in the Pré-aux-Clercs, and perhaps of no very different nature. A deep silence reigned throughout the house ; and a mortal quarter of an hour passed, during which his fancy painted by turns Venus stepping from the tapestry to throw herself into his arms, the Countess de Turgis in her hunting habit, a princess of the blood royal, a gang of assassins, and then—idea more horrid still than this !—an old woman in love with him.

Suddenly, without the least preliminary noise to show that anyone had entered the house, the key turned quickly in the lock ; the door opened and shut, as if automatically, the moment a masked lady had stepped into the room.

Her stature was tall and well proportioned. A gown fitting closely to her bust showed the grace of her figure ;

but neither the tiny foot slippered in white velvet, nor the little hand unluckily covered with an embroidered glove, could give any clear indication of the incognita's age; yet something—magnetic influence, instinct, or what not—made him guess that she was not more than five-and-twenty. Her costume united simplicity, splendour, and elegance.

Mergy rose at once, and bent knee before her. The lady advanced one step, and then said in a sweet voice:

"*Dios os guarde, caballero. Sea V. M. el bien venido.*" [1]

Mergy gave a start of surprise.

"*Habla V. M. español?*" [2]

But he spoke no Spanish, and could hardly understand any.

The lady seemed vexed; but she allowed Mergy to lead her to one of the chairs, in which she sat, motioning to him to take the other. Then she began the conversation in French, but with a foreign accent, which was sometimes very marked, and, as it were, exaggerated, while at other times it did not appear at all.

"Sir, your valiancy has made me forget the reserve customary with my sex. I wished to see so accomplished a cavalier, and I find him none other than repute has asserted."

Mergy blushed and bowed. "Will you, madame," said he, "be so cruel as to preserve that mask, which like an envious cloud hides from me the rays of the sun?" Now he had read this phrase in a book translated from the Spanish.

"Sir Cavalier, if I find your discretion to be of proof, you shall see me more than once face to face; but for to-day you must be content with the pleasures of conversation."

[1] "God keep you, Sir. Welcome."
[2] "Do you speak Spanish?"

" Ah, madame, that pleasure, by its very greatness, makes me long but more violently to see you."

He was kneeling at her feet, and seemed as though he would raise the mask.

" *Poco a' poco,*' Sir Frenchman ! You go too fast. Resume your seat, or I leave you this moment. If you knew who I am and what I dare in order to see you, you would be content with the mere honour that I do you in coming hither."

" Truly, I think your voice is not unknown to me."

" Yet you have never heard it before. Tell me, could you love faithfully a woman who loved you ?"

" Since I have been with you I have felt——"

' " Fair and softly."

" You have never seen me, so you cannot love me.   You
do not know whether I am fair or foul."

" I am sure you are charming."

The incognita withdrew her hand which he had seized,
and lifted it to her mask as though she would take it off.

" But what would you do if you saw before you a woman
fifty years old and frightfully hideous ? "

" That is impossible."

" Yet at fifty one can love still."   She sighed as she spoke,
and the young man shuddered.

" Your charming form, your hand that you are trying in
vain to rob me of, all things prove your youth."

But there was more gallantry than assurance in this
speech.

" Alas ! " she sighed.

Mergy began to be really alarmed.

" Love is not enough for you men," she said ; " you must
have beauty too."   And she sighed once more.

" Let me, I implore you, take off this mask——"

" No, no ! " and she repulsed him briskly.   " Remember
your promise ! "   But then she added in a gayer tone, " I
should run too much risk in unmasking.   I like to see you
at my feet ; and if perchance I were neither young nor fair —
if you thought me neither—you might leave me disconso-
late."

" Show me then but that little hand of yours ! "

She drew off a perfumed glove, and held out to him a
hand as white as snow.

" I know that hand ! " cried he.   " There is but one so fair
in all Paris."

" Indeed ! and whose is that ? "

" A countess's."

" What countess ? "

" The Countess de Turgis."

" Ah ! I know what you mean. Madame de Turgis has white hands enough, thanks to her perfumer's almond paste. But I think I can boast that mine are softer than hers."

All this was said very naturally ; and Mergy, who had thought that he recognized the beautiful countess's voice, grew doubtful, and felt as if he must give up the notion.

" Two instead of one !" thought he. " Have I a fairy godmother ? " And he strove to discover on the lovely hand the mark of a ring which he had seen Madame de Turgis wear. But the fingers, round and of perfect symmetry, showed not the slightest mark of wear, not the faintest trace of being out of shape.

" Madame de Turgis !" again cried the incognita, laughing. " Truly you are kind to take me for her. I trust, thanks to heaven, I have a little the advantage of her !"

" Yet, on my honour, the countess is the most beautiful woman I have ever seen."

" You love her, then ? " asked she sharply.

" Perhaps ; but I beg you, take off your mask, and show me a woman fairer still."

" When I am sure that you love me, then you shall see me face to face."

" Love you ? But, in God's name, how am I to love you without seeing you ? "

" This hand is pretty : fancy my face a match for it."

" Now I *know* you are charming ; for you have just betrayed yourself by dropping the disguise of your voice. I am certain I recognized it !"

" And it is the voice of Madame de Turgis ? " said she, laughing, and with a strong Spanish accent.

" Exactly so."

" A mistake, a mistake of yours, Señor Bernardo! My name is Doña Maria—Doña Maria de——but I will tell you my surname later. I am a lady of Barcelona; my father, who keeps stern watch over me, has been travelling for some time, and I profit by his absence to amuse myself and see the French Court. As for Madame de Turgis, cease, I pray you, to mention that woman to me; I hate her very name! There is no spitefuller lady at Court. And do you not know, too, how she became a widow ?"

" I have heard something."

" Well, then, speak ! What did they tell you ?"

" That, finding her husband paying attentions to her waiting-woman, she seized a poniard, and dealt him such a blow with it that the poor man died a month afterwards."

" And the deed seems horrible to you ?"

" Nay, I confess that I can excuse her. They say she loved her husband ; and I think nobly of jealousy."

" You say that because you think yourself in her presence, but at heart you despise her."

There was a touch of sadness and melancholy in the voice, but it was not now that of Madame de Turgis, and Mergy was completely puzzled.

" What!" said he, "you are Spanish and you do not respect jealousy ?"

" No more of this. What is the black ribbon that you wear round your neck ?"

" 'Tis a relic."

" I thought you were a Protestant."

" So I am, but this relic was given me by a lady, and I wear it in memory of her."

" Ah ! if you wish to please me you will think no more of
ladies. I would fain be more to you than all women. Who
gave you the reliquary ? Madame de Turgis again ? "

" Nay, truly."

" 'Tis false."

" Then you *are* Madame de Turgis ! "

" You have betrayed yourself, Señor Bernardo."

" How ? "

" When I see Madame de Turgis I shall ask how
she came to commit sacrilege by giving a holy thing to a
heretic."

Mergy's puzzlement grew deeper every moment.

" But," she continued, " I want that reliquary. Give it
me ! "

" No : I cannot."

" I will have it. Dare you refuse me ? "

" But I promised to return it to the giver."

" Bah ! a childish promise that ! Promises made to false
women are not binding. Besides, take heed ! 'tis, perchance,
a charm, a dangerous talisman, that you wear. They say
she is a great enchantress."

" I believe not in witchcraft."

" Nor in wizards ? "

" I believe a little in *witches*," and he laid stress on the
last word.

" Listen ! Give me the relic, and perhaps then I will take
off my mask."

" That is her voice this time."

" Once more, will you give me that relic ? "

" I will give it you *back*, if you will doff your mask."

" Ah ! how sick I am of that Turgis of yours ! Love her as
much as you like ; what do I care ? "

She turned on her chair as if irritated; and the satin which veiled her bosom heaved and sank rapidly. For some moments she spoke not. Then suddenly turning once more, she cried in mocking tones, "*Vala me Dios! V. M. no es caballero, es un monge!*" [1]

With a wave of her hand she upset the two tapers that burnt on the table, together with half the bottles and dishes. As the lights went out she tore off her mask, and in the deepest gloom Mergy felt burning lips which sought his, and a pair of arms closely embracing him.

[1] "God forgive me! You are no knight, you are a monk!"

CHAPTER XV.

IN THE DARK.

"By night all cats are grey."

THE clock of a neighbouring church struck four.

"Good heavens! four? I shall hardly have time to reach home before day!"

"Ah, cruel love! you would leave me so soon?"

"I must; but we shall soon see each other again."

"We shall soon see each other? you forget, dearest countess, that I have not seen you yet!"

"Never mind your countess, baby that you are! I am Doña Maria; and when the light comes you will see that I am not she for whom you take me."

"Where is the door? I will call someone."

"No, Bernardo, let me go down by myself; I know the room, and I can find a match."

"Take care not to step on the glass; you broke enough last night."

"I can take care of myself, thank you."

"What have you got there?"

"Ah! 'tis my corset! Holy Virgin! what shall I do? I cut all the laces with your dagger!"

"We must ask the old woman for some more."

"Do not stir, but leave it to me. Farewell, beloved Bernardo!"

The door opened and shut immediately: a long burst of laughter sounding outside. Mergy perceived that his conquest had escaped him, and tried to pursue her. But in the darkness he bumped against the furniture, he entangled himself with garments and curtains, and he never could find the door. Suddenly it opened, and a person entered holding a dark lantern. Mergy seized the lantern-bearer at once.

"Ah!" cried he, with a tender embrace. "I have got you now; you cannot escape me again!"

"Let me alone, M. de Mergy," said a gruff voice. "Is that the way you squeeze people?"

He recognized the crone, and exclaimed, "The devil take you!"

Then he dressed himself without speaking, took up his weapons and his cloak, and left the house in very much the temper of a man who, after drinking fine Malaga wine, swallows by his servant's carelessness a glass of antiscorbutic syrup which has been forgotten for some years in the cellar.

Mergy was cautious enough with his brother. He told

him of a Spanish lady of great beauty, as far as he could judge in the absence of light ; but he did not so much as mention the suspicions which had occurred to him about his incognita.

CHAPTER XVI.

THE CONFESSION.

"*Amphitryon.* No more of this, Alcmena, I beseech you.
Let us be serious."

MOLIÈRE, *Amphitryon.*

TWO days passed without any message from the pretended Spaniard, and on the third the brothers learnt that Madame de Turgis had arrived the day before in Paris, and that she would certainly go to pay her respects to the Queen-Mother in the course of the day. They went at once to the Louvre, and found her in a gallery surrounded by ladies, with whom she was conversing. The sight of Mergy

did not seem to cause her the slightest emotion, nor did the
faintest blush colour her generally pale cheeks ; but as soon
as she saw him, she nodded to him as to an old acquaintance,
and after the usual compliments were exchanged she leant
towards him and whispered :

"I hope your Huguenot obstinacy is a little shaken now.
Miracles were necessary to convert you."

"How so?"

"What! Have you not experienced in your own person
the marvellous effect of the virtue of relics?"

Mergy smiled incredulously.

"The memory of the fair hand which gave me this little
box," said he, "and the love with which it inspired me, no
doubt doubled my strength and my skill."

She laughed ; but shook her finger threateningly at him.

"You are becoming impertinent, master cornet! Do you
know who it is to whom you speak thus?"

As she spoke she drew off her glove to arrange her hair.
Mergy stared at the hand, and from it carried his glance to
the eyes, wide-awake and wicked-looking, of the beautiful
countess. She burst out laughing at his astonished countenance.

"Why do you laugh?" said he.

"If you come to that, why do you look at me with this
astounded air?"

"Pardon me, but for some days past I have been living
in a state of wonder."

"Indeed? That must be interesting. Tell me quickly
some of these wondrous things which have been continually
happening to you."

"I cannot tell you *now* or *here;* besides, I do not forget a
certain Spanish motto which I was taught three days ago."

" What motto is that ? "

" A single word : *Callad.*"

" What does that mean ? "

" Ah, you do not know Spanish," said he, observing her narrowly ; but she bore his examination without the slightest appearance of perceiving any hidden meaning in his words ; and the young man, after fixing his eyes on hers, had in fact to lower them soon in forced recognition of the more potent spirit in those which he had ventured to challenge.

" In my childhood," said she, with an air of complete unconcern, " I knew a few words of Spanish, but I think I have forgotten them now ; so talk French, if you wish me to understand you. What does your motto mean ? "

" It recommends discretion, madame."

" By my faith ! it would be a good motto for our young courtiers, especially if they could manage to suit the deed to the word. But you are very clever, M. de Mergy. Who taught you Spanish ? I will wager that it was a lady."

Mergy looked at her tenderly, and with something of a smirk.

" I know but a word or two of Spanish," said he under his breath ; " and it was love that engraved them on my memory."

" Love ! " repeated the countess mockingly. And as she spoke quite loud, several ladies turned their heads at the word, as if to ask what was the matter.

Mergy, rather piqued at her satire, and annoyed at seeing himself treated thus, drew from his pocket the Spanish letter which he had received from the crone, and offered it to the countess.

" I have no doubt," said he, " that you are as clever as I,

and that you will have no difficulty in construing this
Spanish."

Diane de Turgis snatched the billet, read it, or pretended
to read it, and, laughing consumedly, handed it to the lady
next her.

"Come, Madame de Châteauvieux," said she, "read this
love-letter which M. de Mergy has just received from his
mistress, and which he is good enough, as it appears, to lay
at my feet. The beauty of it is that I know the hand."

"Very likely," said Mergy rather bitterly, but still in a
low tone.

Madame de Châteauvieux read the letter; laughed, and
passed it to a gentleman, who did the same to another; and
in a minute or two everyone in the gallery was acquainted
with the favour which a Spanish lady had shown to Mergy.

When the laughter ceased, the countess demanded of
Mergy whether he thought the lady of the letter pretty.

"On my honour, madame," said he, "I think her not
less pretty than yourself."

"Oh, heavens! what do you say? But you must only
have seen her at night; for I know her well. And faith! I
congratulate you on your good fortune." And she began to
laugh more uncontrollably than ever.

"But, my pretty Diane," said Madame de Châteauvieux,
"why do you not tell us who this Spanish dame is who is
lucky enough to have secured M. de Mergy's heart?"

"Before I name her, I beg you, M. de Mergy, to declare
before these ladies whether you have seen your love by
daylight?"

Mergy felt not a little awkward; and his uneasiness and
vexation were visible on his countenance in a sufficiently
amusing manner. But he held his tongue.

" Not to make mysteries," said the countess, " this note is from the Señora Doña Maria Rodriguez. I know her writing as well as my father's."

" Maria Rodriguez ! " cried all the ladies with a shout of laughter.

Now Doña Rodriguez was a lady of more than fifty summers. She had been a duenna at Madrid ; and I do not know either why she had come to France, or why Marguerite de Valois had given her a place in her household. Perhaps she kept this kind of monster beside her in order to set off her own charms by the contrast ; just as the painters of the time drew on the same canvas the portrait of a beauty and the caricature of her dwarf. But when Doña Rodriguez appeared at the Louvre, she was the butt of all the Court ladies for her starched air and her old-world costume.

Mergy shuddered. He had seen the duenna ; and he remembered with horror that the masked lady had given the name of " Maria." All his memories became entangled ; he was visibly chopfallen, and the laugh redoubled.

" She is a most discreet dame," said Madame de Turgis, " and you could not have made a better choice. She looks quite handsome when she has her false teeth in and her black wig on. Besides, she is certainly not more than sixty."

" She must have bewitched him ! " cried Madame de Châteauvieux.

" Perhaps M. de Mergy is an antiquary ? " asked another lady.

What a pity," said one of the Queen's maidens, sighing low—" what a pity that men will take such ridiculous fancies ! "

Mergy was still trying his best to defend himself, and was cutting a very foolish figure under a shower of ironical congratulations, when the King appeared at the gallery's end. All smiles and jokes ceased at once; the company drew up in rows to let him pass, and silence followed the tumult.

The King was reconducting the Admiral, with whom he

had had a long interview in his cabinet. His hand rested in familiar fashion on the shoulder of Coligny, whose grey beard and black garments contrasted sharply with Charles's youthful mien and his gaily embroidered dress. To see them, men might have said that the young King, with discretion rare on the throne, had chosen the best and wisest of his subjects as a favourite.

As they crossed the gallery, and all eyes were fixed on them, Mergy heard the voice of the countess murmuring

low in his ear, " Do not be angry with me, and do not look
at this till you are outside."

At the same moment there fell into his hat, which he held
in his hand, a sealed paper with something hard inside. He
pocketed it, and ten minutes later, when he had left the
Louvre, he opened it, and found a small key, with the words:
" This key opens my garden gate. To night at ten. I
love you. I shall never be masked for you again, and you
shall at last see Doña Maria and—— DIANE."

The King, after escorting the Admiral to the end
of the gallery, said, " Farewell, father," clasping his
hands. " You know whether I love you ; and I know you
are mine, body and soul." And he followed the words with
a loud laugh. Then, on his way back, he stopped before
Captain George, and said, " To-morrow, after mass, come
and speak to me in my cabinet." He turned his head and
threw a half anxious glance towards the door by which
Coligny had just departed ; then he left the gallery to closet
himself with the Marshal de Retz.

CHAPTER XVII.

THE PRIVATE AUDIENCE.

" Macbeth. Do you find
Your patience so predominant in your nature
That you can let this go ? "

SHAKESPEARE.

CAPTAIN GEORGE betook himself to the Louvre
at the appointed time. He had no sooner given his
name than the usher, raising a door-curtain of tapestry,
introduced him into the King's closet. Charles, who was
sitting by a small table in the attitude of one who writes,
motioned to him with his hand to be quiet, as if he feared
to lose the thread of the ideas which occupied him. So the

captain remained standing in a respectful posture half-a-dozen paces from the table, and had leisure to survey the apartment and to remark its ornaments in detail. They were simple enough, consisting of hardly anything but equipments for the chase hung anyhow about the walls. A fairly good picture of the Virgin, with a great branch of box above it, hung between a long arquebuss and a hunting-horn. The table at which the monarch wrote was covered with papers and books. On the floor a rosary, and a small book of " Hours," lay huddled up with nets and hawks' bells ; while a large greyhound slumbered on a cushion hard by.

Suddenly the King threw down his pen with a gesture of rage and a muttered oath. His head on his breast, he paced the length of the room twice or thrice with ill-measured steps, and then, suddenly halting in front of the captain, he gazed at him in a startled fashion, as if he had not noticed him before.

" Ah! 'tis you!" he cried, with a step backward.

The captain bowed to the ground.

" I am glad to see you. I had something to say to you ——but——" And he stopped.

George, as he waited for the end of the sentence, stood with his mouth slightly open, his neck stretched forward, his left foot some inches in advance of the right—in short, in the exact position, I think, which a painter would give to a figure of Attention. But the King's head dropped once more on his bosom, and he seemed busy with some idea a thousand leagues away from those which he had just been on the point of putting into words. For some minutes there was total silence, and Charles at last sat down and put his hand to his brow as one wearied.

" The deuce is in the rhyme!" cried he, with a stamp and

a clang of the long spurs with which his
boots were garnished. The great hound
woke with a start, and taking the stamp for
a signal to himself, got up, came close to
the King's chair, laid his two paws on the
royal knees, and, lifting his slender head,
which rose far above the King's, opened
his mouth wide and yawned in the most
unceremonious manner. So difficult
is it to teach dogs a courtly mode of
behaviour.

But the King drove away the dog,

who lay down again with a
sigh, and once more, his eyes
meeting the captain's as if by chance,
he said, "Excuse me, George, it is
a——' rhyme which has driven me
to desperation."

The reader may supply an epi-
thet. Charles IX. frequently used
oaths, which were forcible enough in
all conscience, but far from elegant.

" Perhaps I am in your Majesty's way ?" said the captain, with another deep bow.

" Not at all, not at all," said the King, rising and putting his hand on the captain's shoulder familiarly. He smiled as he did it, but his smile was on the lips only, and his eyes, which were far distraught, took no part therein.

" Did the chase the other day tire you ?" asked he at last, evidently finding some difficulty in starting his subject. " The stag made a long fight of it."

" Sire, I should hardly be worthy to command a troop of your Majesty's light horse if a day's hunting like that of the day before yesterday tired me. In the late war M. de Guise used to call me the Albanian, because he never saw me out of the saddle."

" Yes, I have been told that you are a good horseman. But tell me, are you a good shot ?"

" I can use the arquebuss pretty well, sire, though I am far from being your Majesty's equal at it. Such skill is not given to everyone."

" Well, you see that long piece there. Load it with a dozen buckshot, and —— me if at sixty paces one of them goes wide of the breast of the scoundrel you may have taken for mark !"

" Sixty paces is a fair range ; but I would rather not try the experiment personally with a marksman like your Majesty."

" And it would send a ball of the right calibre into a man's body at two hundred," said the King, putting the arquebuss into the captain's hands.

" It seems as good as it is richly mounted," said George, after carefully examining it, and trying the lock.

" I see, brave captain, that you know something about

guns. Take aim with it, that I may see how you go to
work."

The captain obeyed, and Charles went on speaking slowly.
" A pretty tool is an arquebuss ! At a hundred paces, and
with a crook of the finger, thus, one can be sure of ridding
oneself of an enemy ; and neither mail shirt nor corslet will
keep out a good bullet."

I have already said that Charles IX., either from a
trick acquired in youth, or from natural timidity, scarcely
ever looked his interlocutor in the face. But this time he
looked straight at the captain with a singular expression
in his eyes. George dropped his own almost without intending it ; and the King almost immediately did the same.
There was silence for a moment, but George was the first
to break it.

" Still, however adroit a man may be with firearms, lance
and sword are the surer weapons."

" Yes, but the arquebuss——" and Charles smiled oddly.
Then he began again : " They say, George, that the
Admiral has mortally insulted you ? "

" Sire   "

" I know it ; I am certain of it. But I should like you
——I could wish you to tell me the matter yourself."

" Sire, it is true : I was speaking to him of an unlucky
affair in which I had the deepest interest——"

" Your brother's duel ? Faith, 'tis a pretty fellow who
knows how to spit a man neatly ; I honour him for it :
Comminges was a coxcomb and got his deserts. But, death
of my life ! how the devil did old Greybeard find occasion
in this to pick a quarrel with you ? "

" I fear that certain hapless differences of religion, and
my conversion, which I thought had been forgotten——"

" Forgotten ? "

" Your Majesty having set the example of forgetting religious differences, and your Majesty's rare and impartial justice being——"

" Learn, my good fellow, that the Admiral never forgets."

" Sire, I have had occasion to perceive that," and George's face darkened.

" Tell me, captain, what do you mean to do ? "

" I, sire ? "

" Yes : speak frankly."

" Sire, I am too poor a gentleman, and the Admiral is too old a man, for me to challenge him ; and besides, sire," added he with a bow, and an attempt to make good what he thought might seem to the King too bold a speech by a courtly phrase, " if a duel were possible, I should fear to lose your Majesty's favour by it."

" Bah ! " said the King, and he rested his right hand on George's shoulder.

" Luckily," went on the captain, " my honour is not in the Admiral's hands ; and if anyone of my own rank suggested any doubt of it, then I should ask for your Majesty's permission——"

" That means that you will not take revenge on the Admiral himself ? yet the fellow grows terribly insolent."

George opened his eyes in amazement.

" And yet further," continued the King, " he *has* insulted you, has grievously insulted you, may the devil take me ! if they say truth. A gentleman is not a footboy, and there are things which cannot be borne even from a prince."

" But how can I avenge me ? He would think it below his birth to fight with me."

" Perhaps ; but——" and the King lifted the arquebuss, and took aim with it once more.

" Do you understand me ? " said he.

The captain fell back two steps ; for the monarch's gesture was plain enough, and the diabolical expression of his countenance gave it only too clear a comment.

" What ! sire, you would advise me—— ? "

The King struck the butt of the gun violently on the floor, and cried, looking at the captain with angry eyes :

" I advise you ! By the body of God ! I advise you nothing ! "

Not knowing what to answer, George did what many people would have done in his place. He bowed, and looked at the ground.

But the King soon went on in a milder tone :

" Still, if you happened to let fly at him in order to avenge your honour, I cannot say that I should greatly care. By

the Pope's bowels! a gentleman has no more precious
possession than his honour, and there is nothing he may not
do to make it safe and sound. Besides, these Châtillons
are as proud and insolent as the hangman's understrappers.
The rascals would twist my neck, I know, if they could, and
take my place. Why, sometimes when I see the Admiral
my fingers itch to tear his beard out."

But to this flow of language from a man ordinarily sparing
of speech, the captain answered never a word.

"Well!" continued the King, "what in God's name are
you going to do? In your place I would wait for him as he
comes from his accursed meeting-house, and send a good
arquebuss charge from a window into his loins. My cousin
of Guise would be grateful enough to you, by Jove! and you
would have done much for the peace of the kingdom. Do
you not know that this heretic is more king of France than
I am myself? I am sick of it; I tell you frankly what I
think; we must teach the ——— not to touch the honour of a
gentleman. A hole drilled through the skin is fair pay for
a wound given to honour."

"A gentleman's honour is not mended but ended by
assassination."

The answer came on the King like a thunderbolt. Motionless, his hands stretched towards the captain, he still clutched
the arquebuss which he had seemed to offer as an instrument
of vengeance. His lips were bloodless and half-parted, and
his haggard eyes, fixed on those of George, seemed at once
to exercise and undergo a horrid fascination. At last the
gun dropped from his quivering grasp, and echoed as it fell
on the floor. The captain darted at once to pick it up, and
the King sat down in his chair, dropping his head in his
sombre fashion on his breast, while the twitching of his

eyebrows and his mouth gave evidence of the struggle which was going on in his heart.

"Captain," said he after a long silence, "where is your troop of light horse?"

"At Meaux, sire."

"In a day or two you will join it and bring it yourself to Paris. In——yes, in a day or two you will have your orders; farewell!" and his voice still rang harsh and angrily. The captain bowed deeply, and Charles, pointing to the closet door, informed him that his audience was finished.

He was departing backwards with the usual ceremonial bows, when the King, rising sharply, seized his arm——

"Keep your mouth shut at least! You understand?"

George bowed once more, and laid his hand on his heart. As he left the room he heard the King harshly calling his greyhound, and cracking his dogwhip, as if inclined to vent his wrath on the innocent animal.

As soon as he was at home the captain wrote the following missive, which he conveyed to the Admiral: "One who loves you not, but loves honour, bids you beware of the Duke of Guise.

and, it may be, of someone mightier still. Your life is in danger."

But the letter produced no effect on Coligny's dauntless soul. All know that shortly afterwards, on the 22nd of August, 1572, he was wounded with an arquebuss-shot by a wretch named Maurevel, who received from the deed the nickname of " The King's Butcher."

CHAPTER XVIII.

THE CATECHUMEN.

*" 'Tis pleasing to be schooled in a
strange tongue
By female lips and eyes."*
LORD BYRON, *Don Juan*,
canto ii.

WHEN two lovers are very cautious, sometimes a whole week or more passes before the public is admitted to their secret. At the end of that time prudence gives herself a holiday; precaution begins to appear ridiculous. Somebody intercepts a glance with little difficulty, construes it with still less, and then all is known.

D D

Thus no long time passed before the connection of the Countess de Turgis and the younger Mergy ceased to be a secret for Catherine's Court. A crowd of convincing proofs would have been enough to open even blind eyes. For instance, Madame de Turgis usually wore lilac ribbons; and rosettes of lilac ribbons adorned Bernard's sword-hilt, the skirts of his doublet, and his shoes. The countess had made no secret of her dislike for a beard, and her liking for a smartly turned-up moustache; now for some short time Mergy's chin had been always carefully shaved, while his moustache—ferociously curled, stiffly pomaded, and combed with a leaden comb—described a crescent, the points of which soared considerably above his nose. And people even had the impudence to say that a certain gentleman, who had occasion to go forth very early, and was passing through the Rue des Assis, had seen the countess's garden gate open, and a man come forth, whom, notwithstanding the fact that his face was completely enveloped in his cloak, he had had no difficulty in recognizing as the Seigneur de Mergy.

But the most convincing proof of all, and the most surprising to the world, was the sight of the young Huguenot—the pitiless derider of all the ceremonies of the Catholic faith—assiduously frequenting the churches, never missing a procession, and even dipping his fingers in holy water, which a day or two earlier he would have regarded as hideous sacrilege. Men whispered that Diane had gained a soul for heaven; and young gentlemen of the Protestant faith made it known that they were not indisposed to consider the question of conversion seriously, if, instead of Capuchins and Franciscans, missionaries to them were selected from youthful and pious beauties like Madame de Turgis.

Yet Bernard was a long way from being converted. Certainly he went to church with the countess ; but then he kept at her side, and never ceased whispering in her ear during the whole mass, to the great scandal of the faithful. By this means he not only escaped listening to the service himself, but also prevented devout persons from attending to it as they ought to have done. As for processions, it is well known that in those days they were mere pleasure parties, as full of amusement as a masquerade. And lastly, Mergy had given up his scruple about dipping his fingers in holy water, simply because it gave him the occasion of publicly squeezing a pretty hand which never touched his without a quiver. However, if he kept his faith, he had to fight stoutly for it ; and Diane had all the greater advantage in her controversies with him, that she generally chose, for the purpose of theological discussion, the particular moments when it was hardest for Mergy to refuse her anything.

" Dear Bernard," said she one evening, resting her head on her lover's shoulder, while she twined her long black tresses round his neck "dear Bernard, you were at church to-day with me. Did that beautiful sermon produce no effect on your heart ? Will you always be stubborn ? "

" Ah, dearest ! how can you believe that a whining Capuchin can do what you have not done with your sweet voice, and with religious arguments so well reinforced by my Diane's loving looks ? "

" Sinner ! I should like to strangle you ! " And pulling one of her locks a little tighter, she drew him still closer to herself.

" Do you know how I spent sermon-time ? " asked he. " In counting the pearls in your hair. Only see how you have spilt them about the room ! "

"I knew it! You did not listen to the sermon! It is always the same story. Ah!" said she a little sadly, "well do I see that you love me not as I love you. If you did, you would have been converted long ago."

"But, Diane! why this eternal argument? Let us leave it to the Sorbonne doctors and to our preachers; and let us pass our own time better!"

"Let me go! If only I could save you, how happy I should be! Why, my Bernardo, to do that, I would double the number of years that I shall have to spend in purgatory!"

He smiled, and pressed her in his arms; but she repulsed him with an air of ineffable sadness.

"*You* would not do that for me, Bernard. You care nothing for the risk my soul runs when I give myself thus to you!" And the tears suffused her beautiful eyes.

" Dearest love, do you not know that for love's sake many sins are forgiven ? "

" Yes, I know that. But if I could save you, all my sins would be forgiven me : all those we have done —all those we may do hereafter— *all* would be pardoned. Nay, our very sins themselves would have been but the instruments of our salvation ! "

And as she spoke she tightened her arms round him with all her strength ; yet the passionate exaltation with which she spoke had, in the particular situation, something so comical about it, that Mergy felt some difficulty in preventing a burst of laughter at this singular fashion of exhorting.

" Let us put our conversion off a little longer, my Diane," said he. " When we are both old ; when we are too old to love, then——"

" Ah, wicked love ! you drive me to despair ! Why this diabolical smile on your lips ? Do you think I long to kiss them when they look like that ? "

" But you see I am not smiling now."

" Come, be quiet ; and tell me, *querido Bernardo*, did you read the book I gave you ? "

" Yes. I finished it yesterday."

" Well, what do you think of it ? There is reasoning for you !—reasoning to shut the mouth of the infidel ! "

" Your book, my beloved Diane, is only a farrago of nonsense and irrelevance. It is the foolishest that has yet come from your Popish press ; and I will bet that, boldly as you speak of it, you have never read it."

" No," she answered, blushing a little ; " I have not read it yet. But I am sure it is full of truth and reason. I do not want any other proof than the persistence of the Huguenots in crying it down."

"Then shall I, to amuse you, go through it Bible in hand?"

"Oh! never, Bernard! Mercy on me, I am not a Bible-reader, like you heretics. I will not have you weaken my faith. And besides, you would only lose your labour. You Huguenots are always so desperately ready with your learning; you throw it in our teeth when you argue; and we poor Catholics, who have not read Aristotle and the Scriptures like you, do not know what to answer."

"That is because you choose to believe at any cost, without giving yourselves the trouble to find out whether belief is reasonable or not. Now we at least study our religion before defending it, and, above all, before trying to make converts of others."

"I would I had the eloquence of Father Giron, the Franciscan."

"He is a fool and a babbler. But he might shout as loud as he liked six years ago in a public discussion; our minister Houdart put him down."

"A story—a heretic story!"

"What? Do you not know that in the course of the debate great drops of perspiration were seen to fall from the good father's brow on the Chrysostom he held in his hand? Whereon a wit made these verses——"

"I will not hear them! Do not poison my ears with your heresy. Bernard! my beloved Bernard! I adjure you listen not to all these ministers of Satan, who deceive you and lead you hellwards. I implore you, save your soul and come back to the Church!" And as, despite her entreaties, she still read on her lover's lips the smile of unbelief—"If you love me," she cried, "renounce for me, for my sake, your damnable beliefs."

"I could more easily, dearest, renounce my life for you than what reason shows me to be true. How can you wish even love to prevent my believing that two and two make four?"

"Cruel!" she cried. But Bernard had an infallible secret for putting a stop to discussions of this kind, and he employed it.

"Alas! dear Bernardo," said the countess in a languishing voice, when dawning day made it necessary for Mergy to leave her, "I peril my soul for you, and yet, I see too well, I shall not have the consolation of saving yours."

"Come, come, my angel, Father Giron will give us both a right absolution *in articulo mortis.*"

CHAPTER XIX.

THE FRANCISCAN.

"A monk in the cloister
Is not worth an oyster :
But once set him free
He is worth thirty-three."

THE day after the marriage of Marguerite with the King of Navarre, Captain George, by the orders of the Court, left Paris in order to take the command of his

[1] In original

"Monachus in claustro
Non valet ova duo ;
Sed quando est extra
Bene valet triginta." *Translator's Note.*

E E

troop of light horse, then garrisoning Meaux. His brother
bade him farewell cheerfully enough ; and, hoping to see him
again before the end of the merrymaking, made up his mind
to keep house by himself for some days. He was sufficiently busy with Madame de Turgis not to be desperately
afraid of a little solitude, for he was never at home by night,
and took his sleep by day.

On Friday, the 22nd of August, 1572, the Admiral was
severely wounded by an arquebuss-shot from a scoundrel of
the name of Maurevel. And as public rumour set this
cowardly attempt at assassination to the credit of the Duke
de Guise, that lord quitted Paris the next day, as if to be
out of reach of the complaints and the threats of the
reformers. The King seemed at first anxious to prosecute
him with the utmost severity ; but he made no opposition to
his return, which was to be marked by the terrible massacre
of the 24th.

It happened that a goodly company of well-mounted
young Protestant gentlemen, after paying a visit of inquiry
to the Admiral, spread themselves about the streets with
the intention of searching out Guise or his friends and
picking a quarrel if they met them. Yet at first things
went quietly enough. The populace, alarmed at their numbers, or perhaps biding another time, were silent as they
passed, and heard unmoved their cries of " Death to the
Admiral's assassins !" and " Down with the Guisards !"

At the corner of a street some dozen Catholic youth of
quality, among them more than one follower of the House
of Guise, suddenly faced the Protestant party. A serious
squabble seemed likely ; but nothing of the sort happened.
The Catholics, perhaps from prudence, perhaps acting under
orders, made no answer to the insulting cries of the

Huguenots ; and a young man of good appearance, who was at their head, advanced towards Mergy, bowed to him politely, and said in a familiar and friendly tone, "Good day, M. de Mergy. You have seen M. de Châtillon, of course ? How is he ? Have they caught the assassin ?"

The two parties halted, and Mergy, recognizing the Baron de Vaudreuil, returned his salutation and answered his questions. Other remarks were exchanged between individuals on both sides ; and as they were brief, the parting took place without a quarrel. The Catholics yielded the crown of the causeway, and each went his way.

Vaudreuil had held Mergy back for some time, so that he was separated from his companions. As they parted, Vaudreuil looked at Mergy's saddle, and said, " Take care ! Unless I mistake, your nag is ill-girthed. Look to it." Mergy dismounted and adjusted the girths ; but he was scarcely in the saddle again when he heard a sharp trot behind him. He turned his head, and saw a young man whose face he did not know, but who had been one of the party they had just met.

"—— me !" cried the newcomer, addressing him. " I would I could meet, man to man, one of the fellows who just now cried ' Down with the Guisards.' "

" You need not go far to find one, sir," answered Mergy. " What can I do to oblige you ?"

" Ah ! Are you one of the rascals ?"

Mergy drew at once, and struck the Guises' friend over the face with the flat of his sword. He seized a holster pistol and fired it point-blank at Mergy. Luckily it flashed in the pan, and Diane's lover, replying with a stout sword-blow on his foe's head, stretched him, bathed in his blood, at his horse's feet. Instantly the populace, who had hitherto been neutral, took the side of the wounded man. The young Huguenot was assailed with sticks and stones; and as resistance against such numbers was hopeless, he set spurs to his steed and gallopped off. But just as he tried to cut a corner too sharply his horse fell, and threw him without hurting him, but also without giving him a chance of mounting again quickly enough to save himself from being surrounded by the enraged mob. So he set his back to the wall, and for some time kept off those who came within sword reach. But a mighty bludgeon blow having shivered his blade, he was thrown to the ground, and would have been torn in pieces if a cordelier, throwing himself in front of those who were pressing on, had not covered him with his own body.

" What are you doing, children ? " cried he. " Let the man go! He is not to blame."

" 'Tis a Huguenot!" yelled a hundred furious voices.

" Well! give him time to repent. He can still do so."

The hands which clutched Mergy let him go : he rose, and picking up his broken sword, prepared to sell his life dear if he should have to sustain a new attack.

" Let the man live ! " repeated the monk, " and be patient. The Huguenots will all come to mass before long."

" Patience? patience?" echoed some voices angrily. " We have heard that for a long time now, and yet every Sunday in their conventicles their psalm-singing offends good Christians ! "

" Well," said the monk cheerfully, " do ye not know the proverb, ' The owl sings long, but he grows hoarse at last ?' Let them bray a little more ; ye shall soon, by the grace of our Lady of August, hear them sing mass in Latin. But as for this young misbeliever, give him to me. I'll make a good

Christian of him. Away with you, and don't burn the roast in your haste to eat."

The crowd dispersed grumbling, but offering Mergy not the least insult. They even caught his horse for him.

"This is the first time in my life, father," said he, "that it has given me pleasure to see that cloth of yours. Believe me that I am grateful, and deign to take this purse."

"If you mean it for the poor, my boy, I will take it. But know that I take an interest in you. Your brother is my friend, and I wish you well. Become a convert at once: come with me, and your business shall soon be done."

"I thank you for the offer, father, but I have not the least wish to be converted. How do you know me? What is your name?"

"They call me Brother Lubin, and I think, young rogue, I have seen you pretty often hanging about a certain house. But mum for that. Tell me, M. de Mergy, do you believe now that a monk can do a good deed?"

"I will publish your generous conduct everywhere, Brother Lubin."

"Yet you will not quit meeting for mass?"

"Once more, no; and I will never go to church except to hear your sermons."

"You are evidently a man of taste."

"Yes; and an admirer of yours to boot."

"Then I am sincerely sorry that you persist in your heresy. I have warned you; I have done what I could; what will come must come of it. I wash my hands. Farewell, my child!"

"Farewell, father!" and Mergy, mounting his horse, made his way back to his lodgings a little bruised, but uncommonly well satisfied with having got so cheaply out of so awkward an affair.

CHAPTER XX.

THE LIGHT HORSEMEN.

" *Jaffier.* He amongst us
That spares his father, brother, or his friend,
Is damned."
OTWAY, *Venice Preserved.*

ON the evening of the 24th of August a squadron of light horse entered Paris by the gate of Saint Antoine, the dusty boots and uniforms of the troopers showing that they had had a long ride. Their bronzed countenances

were lighted up by the last glow of daylight; and upon
these countenances might be read the vague anxiety which
is felt at the approach of a thing, as yet not fully known,
but suspected to be of evil nature.

The troop rode slowly towards a wide expanse of ground,
free from houses, which stretched alongside of the old palace
of the Tournelles. There their captain bade them halt,
sent out a dozen men under his cornet to reconnoitre, and
himself posted sentinels at the mouth of each adjoining
street, with matches burning, as if in presence of the enemy.
This unusual precaution taken, he returned to the front of
his lines.

"Sergeant!" cried he, in a harsher and more imperious
tone than was his wont: and an old trooper, his hat adorned
with a gold stripe, and wearing an embroidered scarf,
respectfully approached his chief.

"Have all the troopers matches?"

"Yes, captain."

"Are the powder-horns full? Is there store of bullets?"

"Yes, captain."

"It is well." And he walked his mare along the front of
his little force, the sergeant following him a horse's length
in the rear. He had perceived his captain's ill-temper, and
was shy of addressing him; but at last he took courage.

"Captain," said he, "may I give the men leave to feed
their horses? you know that they have not eaten since the
morning."

"No."

"Not even a handful of oats? It would not take long."

"Not a horse is to be disbridled."

"Because if they are to have work to-night—as men say
—perhaps then ——"

The officer made a gesture of impatience. "To your post!" said he drily, and as he continued his promenade the sergeant returned to the midst of the soldiers.

"Well, sergeant, is it true? What is going to be done? What is up? What does the captain say?"

A score of questions at once were addressed to him by old soldiers, whom long service and old habit privileged to use this liberty with their superior officer.

"We shall see fine doings," said the sergeant in the important tone of a man who knows more than he says.

"How? how?"

"We are not to take the bridles off; not for a minute. For who knows? we may be needed any moment."

"Aha! there is going to be a fight then?" said the trumpeter. "With whom, an't please you?"

"With whom?" said the sergeant, repeating the question to give himself time to meditate an answer. "A pretty question, faith! With whom would you fight except the King's enemies?"

"Yes; but who are these enemies of the King?" continued the obstinate questioner.

"The King's enemies! he does not know who the King's enemies are," cried the sergeant, shrugging his shoulders compassionately.

"The Spaniards are the King's enemies," said a trooper; "but they can hardly have come up like this, in a cloud of darkness, without anyone knowing it."

"Hah!" retorted another, "I know plenty of enemies of the King who are not Spaniards."

"Bertrand is right," said the sergeant, "and I know whom he means."

"Who are they?"

"The Huguenots," said Bertrand. "One need not be a wizard to see that. Everybody knows that the Huguenots got their religion from Germany; and I am sure the Germans are our enemies, for I have often exchanged pistol-shots with them—notably at St. Quentin, where they fought like devils."

"That is all very fine," said the trumpeter, "but peace has been made with them, and there was fuss enough about it to make one remember it."

"A proof that they are not our enemies," said a young trooper, more richly dressed than the rest, "is that the Count de la Rochefoucauld is to head the light horse in the war which we are going to wage in Flanders. Now everybody knows that La Rochefoucauld is of the religion. Deuce take me if he is not of it from head to foot, for he wears spurs *à la Condé* and a hat *à la Huguenote*."

"A plague on him!" cried the sergeant. "You do not know, Merlin; you had not joined then. But it was La Rochefoucauld who commanded the ambush which nearly finished us off at La Robraye in Poitou. He is a wily rascal that!"

"And he says," added Bertrand, "that a squadron of Reiters is more than a match for a squadron of light horse. I am as sure of it as that yon horse is a roan. I heard it from one of the Queen's pages."

His audience showed signs of wrath; but this gave way soon to their curiosity to know against whom the warlike preparations and the unusual measures of precaution which they saw were being taken.

"Is it true, sergeant," asked the trumpeter, "that there was an attempt to kill the King yesterday?"

"I will bet that 'twas these brutes of heretics."

"The host at the Cross of St. Andrew, where we break-fasted," said Bertrand, "told us how they tried to put an end to the mass."

"In that case we could eat meat every day," said Merlin with much philosophy. "Bacon for bean soup; there is not much to complain of in that."

"Yes; but if the Huguenots rule the roast, the first thing they will do will be to send all our light horse troops packing, and put dogs of German Reiters in our place."

"If that be so, I will not be shy of skin-cutting as far as they are concerned. Death of my life! it makes me a good Catholic again! But tell us, Bertrand, since you have served with the Protestants, is it true that the Admiral gave his troopers only eight sous a day?"

"Not a denier more, the stingy old Jew! so I left him after one campaign."

"How cross the captain is to-day," said the trumpeter. "He, so good a fellow generally, and so ready to talk with the men, has not opened his lips the whole journey."

"The news vexes him," said the sergeant.

"What news?"

"Why, what the Huguenots mean to do."

"The civil war is going to begin again," said Bertrand.

"So much the better for us," said Merlin, who always took things on their cheerful side. "There will be knocks to give, villages to burn, and Huguenot girls to tousle."

"It seems as though they were trying to play their old Amboise trick again," said the sergeant; "and that is why we have been sent for. We will set that matter right enough."

At this moment the cornet returned with his detachment,

and, coming close to the captain, whispered to him, while his
men joined their companions.

"By my beard!" said one of the reconnoitring party, "I
do not know what is going on to-day in Paris. We have
not seen so much as a cat in the streets; while, to make
amends, the Bastille is full of troops. I saw the Swiss pikes
in the courtyard as thick as standing corn!"

"There were some five hundred of them," said another.

"What is certain," said the first speaker, "is that the
Huguenots tried to kill the King, and that in the tussle the
Admiral was wounded by the great Duke of Guise's own
hand."

"Ah, the scoundrel! Well done, Guise!" cried the
sergeant.

"And the fact is," added the trooper, "the Swiss were
saying, in their devil's jargon, that the heretics have been
put up with too long in France."

"For some time past they have certainly been giving
themselves airs," said Merlin.

"A man would say they had beaten us at Jarnac and
Montcontour, to judge by their swashing and swaggering."

"They want," said the trumpeter, "to eat the meat and
leave us the bone."

"It is time," quoth another, "that good Catholics should
curry their hides for them."

"For my part," said the sergeant, "if the King said to
me, 'Kill me these rascals!' may I be reduced to the ranks
if I would wait for him to say it twice!"

"But, Belle-Rose, tell us what the cornet has done?"
asked Merlin.

"He spoke with some kind of Swiss officer; but I could
not hear what he said. It must have been something

interesting, for he kept crying out, ' *Ah, mon Dieu! ah! mon Dieu!* ' "

"Look! here are riders coming up at full gallop. They must be bringing us orders."

"There are but two, meseems; and the captain and the cornet are going to meet them."

Two horsemen were in fact riding rapidly towards the squadron of light cavalry. One, richly dressed and wearing a feathered hat and a green scarf, bestrode a charger. His companion was fat, and short, and squat; he was dressed in a black gown, and carried a large wooden crucifix.

"We are going to fight, for certain," said the sergeant. "They have sent us a chaplain to confess the wounded."

"It is not very pleasant to fight on an empty stomach!" muttered Merlin.

The two horsemen slackened the pace of their steeds, so that on reaching the captain they might halt them without difficulty.

"I kiss M. de Mergy's hands," said the man in the green scarf. "Does he recognize his servant, Thomas de Maurevel?"

The captain was ignorant of Maurevel's latest crime, and knew him only as the assassin of the brave Mouy. He replied very drily:

"I do not know M. de Maurevel; but I suppose that you have come to inform us at last why we are here?"

"The business, sir, is to save our good King and our holy religion from the danger which threatens them."

"What is that danger?" asked George scornfully.

"The Huguenots have conspired against his Majesty; but their guilty plots have been discovered in time, thank God, and all good Christians meet to-night to cut them off in their sleep."

"As the Midianites were cut off by Gideon the mighty," said the man in the black gown.

"What do I hear?" cried Mergy, shuddering with horror.

"The citizens are in arms," went on Maurevel; "the Gardes Françaises and three thousand Swiss are in the town. We are nearly sixty thousand strong. At midnight the signal will be given, and the ball will open."

"Cut-throat villain! What base imposture are you talking? The King does not order murders—the most he does is to reward them."

But as he spoke George remembered the strange conversation he had a day or two before with the King.

"No violence, Sir Captain. If the King's service did not demand all my care I should have an answer for your insults. Listen to me. I come, sent by his Majesty, to desire that you will accompany me with your squadron. The Rue Saint Antoine and the adjoining district are assigned to us, and I bring you an exact list of the persons whom we must despatch. The reverend Father Malebouche will deliver an exhortation to your people, and will distribute among them white crosses, such as all Catholics will wear, lest in the darkness the faithful should be taken for heretics."

"And I am expected to lend my hand to cut the throats of sleeping men?"

"Are you a Catholic, and do you acknowledge Charles IX. as your King? Do you know the writing of the Marshal de Retz, to whom you owe obedience?" And Maurevel handed him a paper which he had in his belt.

Mergy called a trooper, and by the light of a straw torch kindled from an arquebuss-match he read a regular order enjoining upon Captain de Mergy in the King's name to support the civil guard with armed forces, and to put himself under the orders of M. de Maurevel for a purpose which the said Maurevel would explain to him. A schedule to this order contained a string of names, with the heading "List of the heretics to be put to death in the Quarter of Saint Antoine." By the light of the torch burning in the trooper's hands all the cavalry could see the deep emotion which this order, unknown to them as yet, produced on their leader.

"My troopers will never do the work of assassins!" said George, throwing the paper back in Maurevel's face.

"There is no question of assassination," said the priest coolly. "The matter concerns heretics; and what is to be done is to execute justice on them."

"Good people!" cried Maurevel, raising his voice and addressing himself to the horsemen, "the Huguenots design the death of the King and the Catholics. We must anticipate them. To-night we shall kill them all in their sleep; and the King grants you the pillage of their houses."

A shout of savage joy ran along the lines: "Long live the King!" "Death to the Huguenots!"

"Silence in the ranks!" thundered the captain. "No one but I has the right to give orders to these troopers. Comrades, this wretch's words cannot be true, and had the King himself ordered it, my troopers would never slay defenceless men."

The soldiers were silent, but Maurevel and his companion shouted together, "Long live the King!" "Death to the Huguenots!" And the troopers an instant later echoed "Long live the King!" "Death to the Huguenots!"

"Well, captain, will you obey?" said Maurevel.

"I am no longer captain!" cried George, tearing off his collar and scarf, the insignia of his rank.

"Seize the traitor!" shouted Maurevel, drawing his sword. "Kill the rebel who disobeys his King!"

But not a soldier dared to lift hand against his chief. George struck Maurevel's sword out of his hand, but instead of stabbing him with his own he merely smote him on the face with the hilt so forcibly that he unhorsed him. Then he cried out to the squadron, "Farewell, cowards! I thought my men were soldiers, but they are only assassins. For you, Alphonse," turning to the cornet, "if you care to be captain, here is your chance. Put yourself at the head of these brigands."

And with these words he set spurs to his horse and gallopped away towards the centre of the city. The cornet followed him for a stride or two; but soon he slackened his horse's pace, then fell into a walk, and at last halted, wheeled round, and rejoined the troop, no doubt reflecting that his captain's advice, though given in a moment of wrath, was none the less good to follow. Maurevel, still dizzy from the blow he had received, remounted cursing; while the monk, lifting his crucifix, exhorted the soldiers not to give quarter to a single Huguenot, but to drown heresy in its own blood. They had been staggered for a moment by their captain's reproaches; but, relieved of his presence, and seeing before them an alluring prospect of plunder, they brandished their sabres over their heads, and swore to do whatsoever Maurevel bade them.

CHAPTER XXI.

A LAST ATTEMPT.

"Soothsayer. Beware the ides of March."
SHAKESPEARE, *Julius Cæsar.*

THAT same evening, at the usual hour, Mergy left his house, and, well wrapped up in a stone-coloured cloak, his hat pulled over his eyes, he bent his steps with all due discreetness towards the countess's abode. He had scarcely made half-a-dozen steps when he met the surgeon Ambrose

Paré, whom he knew as having been a patient of his while he was wounded. Paré was evidently coming from the Hotel de Châtillon, and Mergy, after making himself known, asked him news of the Admiral.

"He is better," said the leech. "The wound is kindly, and the patient's general health is excellent. With God's grace he will get well. I hope that the draught I have prescribed for him this evening will do him good and give him a quiet night."

A man of the lower class who happened to be passing heard them mention the Admiral's name. As soon as he was far enough off to risk an insolence without fear of punishment, he shouted, "Your devil of an Admiral will dance a jig at Montfaucon before long!" and ran off at full speed.

"The rascal!" said Mergy. "'Tis pity that our great Admiral should be obliged to dwell in a town so full of his enemies."

"Luckily his hotel is well garrisoned," said the surgeon. "I left the stairs crowded with soldiers, who were lighting their matches. Ah, Monsieur de Mergy, these townsfolk love us not. But it is late, and I must return to the Louvre."

They parted, wishing each other good evening, and Mergy went on his way, absorbed in rose-coloured reflections which soon made him forget all about the Admiral and the hatred of the Papists. Yet he could not help noticing a singular bustle in the streets of Paris, which were seldom much frequented so soon after nightfall. Now he met porters carrying burdens of unusual shape, which, dark as it was, he could not but take for bundles of pikes; now it was a detachment of soldiers marching in silence, with ported arms and lighted matches ; elsewhere windows were opening, figures showing themselves for a moment, and retiring at once.

"Ho! good fellow," cried he to a porter, "where are you carrying weapons so late ?"

"To the Louvre, fair sir! for to-night's entertainment," said the man.

"Comrade," next said Mergy to a sergeant in command of a patrol, "where are you going armed in that fashion ?"

"To the Louvre, fair sir! for to-night's entertainment."

"What! sir page ? you are the King's man, are you not ? Where are you and your fellows taking these chargers harnessed for battle ?"

"To the Louvre, fair sir! for to-night's entertainment."

"To-night's entertainment!" said Mergy to himself. "It seems as if everybody except myself were in the secret. However, it matters little. The King can amuse himself without me, and I have little curiosity to see his entertainment."

Somewhat farther on, he noticed a man in shabby clothes, who kept stopping before certain houses and marking the doors with a cross in white chalk.

"What! my good man," said he, "are you a billet-master that you are marking doors like that ?" But the stranger disappeared without making any answer.

As he turned from one street into another, that where the countess lived, he nearly ran into a man, wrapped like himself in a large cloak, who was turning the same corner in the opposite direction. Dark as it was, and anxious as both appeared to be to preserve their incognito, they recognized each other at once.

"Good evening, M. de Béville," said Mergy, holding out his hand.

In order to give him his own, Béville seemed to fumble under his cloak; he shifted something heavy which he was carrying from his right hand to his left, and as he did it the cloak flew a little open.

"Hail! valiant champion, delight of ladies!" said Béville. "I bet that my noble friend is in luck to-night!"

"And you, my good sir? There must be some jealous husbands in your neighbourhood; for unless I am very much mistaken, you have a mail shirt on your shoulders, and what you have under your cloak looks remarkably like a pair of pistols."

"One must be prudent, Monsieur Bernard," said Béville; "one must be very prudent." And as he spoke he re-arranged his cloak carefully, so as to conceal the weapons he was carrying.

"I am very sorry indeed not to be able to offer you my help and sword to-night to keep the street and stand sentinel at your lady's door," said Mergy. "It is impossible now, but on every possible opportunity you may reckon on me."

"No; you cannot come with me to-night, M. de Mergy," said Béville, and as he said this he smiled oddly.

"Well then; good luck and good-bye."

"I wish *you* good luck, too," said Béville, and again there was a certain emphasis in his way of speaking.

They parted, and Mergy had gone some steps further when he heard Béville call him. He turned back and saw him also returning.

"Is your brother in Paris?" said Béville.

"No; but I expect him every day. Ah, but tell me, do you make one in 'to-night's entertainment?'"

" To-night's entertainment ? "

" Yes ; everyone says that there is going to be a great entertainment at Court to-night."

Béville muttered something between his teeth.

" Good-bye, once more," said Mergy; " I am rather in a hurry, and—you know what I mean."

" Listen ! listen ! only a word," cried Béville ; " I cannot let you go without one word of advice, which comes from a true friend."

" What is that ? "

" Do not go to *her* to-night ; believe me, you will thank me to-morrow."

" Is that your advice ? Then I do not understand you. Who is *she* ? "

" Bah ! you know what I mean. If you are wise, cross the river to-night, and at once."

" Is this the joke," said Mergy, " to which you were leading up all this time ? "

" Not in the least. I never was more serious. Cross the Seine, I tell you. If the devil is too strong for you, go to the Rue Saint Jacques, near the Jacobin Convent. Two doors off you will see a large wooden crucifix nailed on the wall of a mean-looking house. The sign is an odd one for the business—but never mind that. Knock, and you will find a very obliging old lady, who will receive you well for my sake. Go, I say, and get reasonable on the other side of the Seine. Mother Brulard has divers pretty and well-bred nieces. You understand me ? "

" You are really too good. I kiss your hands."

" No, no ! pray take the advice I give you. On the word of a gentleman you will not be sorry."

" A thousand thanks : I will avail myself of it another

time. To night I am expected." And Mergy began to step forward.

"Cross the Seine, brave friend ; that is my last word. If you come to harm by neglecting my advice I wash my hands of it."

Béville's voice was so unusually serious that it struck Mergy, who caught hold of him, though he had already turned away. "What the devil do you mean ? Pray speak plainly, M. de Béville, and drop riddles."

"My dear fellow, probably I ought not to speak so plainly as I do. But *cross the water before midnight*, and God be with you."

"But——"

But Béville was far away as he said it. Mergy made as though to follow him, but soon, ashamed of wasting time which might be so much better employed, he retraced his steps, and neared the garden where he had to enter. He was obliged to walk up and down for some time, to give certain passers-by (who he feared might be somewhat surprised at seeing him enter a garden gate at such an hour) time to disappear. The night was fine ; a soft breeze had allayed the heat, and the moon alternately dipped into and emerged from faint white clouds. It was a night made for love.

At last the street was clear for a minute : he opened the garden gate and closed it again noiselessly. His heart beat fast ; but he only thought of the joy awaiting him with his Diane, and all the sinister fancies which Béville's strange words had awakened were soon distant. He stepped on tiptoe to the house, where a lamp burnt behind a red curtain at a half-opened window. It was the appointed signal, and in a moment he was within his mistress's oratory.

She was half-lying, half sitting, on a low couch covered

with deep blue damask; and her dark and dishevelled tresses covered the whole of the pillow on which her head rested. Her eyes were closed, and she seemed to be keeping them so with some effort. The room was lighted by a single lamp of silver hanging from the ceiling, which threw its whole light on the pale face and glowing lips of Diane de Turgis. She was not asleep, but she looked as though she were suffering from a painful

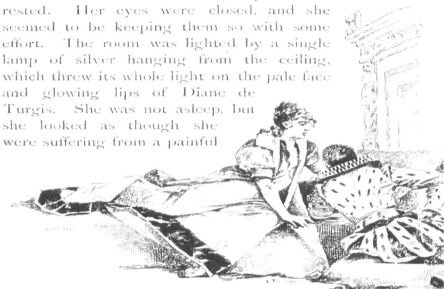

nightmare. Mergy's boots had no sooner creaked on the floor of the oratory than she raised her head, opened her eyes and her mouth, shuddered, and scarcely checked a shriek of terror.

"Did I frighten you, my angel?" said Mergy, kneeling beside her, and stooping over the cushion on which the fair countess had allowed her head once more to drop.

"Thank God," said she, "you are here at last!"

"Am I late? It is still not nearly midnight."

"Ah, do not touch me, Bernard! Did anyone see you enter?"

"No one. But what is the matter with you, love? Why do these sweet little lips shun mine?"

" Ah, Bernard, if you only knew ! Oh, pray do not torment me ! I am horribly ill ; my head aches terribly— my brows are on fire ! "

" Poor darling ! "

" Sit down close to me ; and, I beg you, ask nothing of me to-night ! I am very ill ! " And she hid her lovely face in one of the sofa cushions, letting a moan of anguish escape. Then suddenly she raised herself on her elbows, shook off the thick tresses which covered her face, and grasping Mergy's hand placed it on her own temples, where he felt the violent throbbing of the veins. " Your hand is cool it does me good," said she.

" Dearest Diane," answered he, kissing the burning brow, " how I wish I could take the headache in your stead ! "

" Ah, yes ; and *I* wish—— But put the tips of your fingers on my eyelids ; it will soothe me. I think if I could weep, I should suffer less ; but I can shed no tear."

There was a long silence, interrupted only by the irregular and heavy breathing of the countess. Mergy, kneeling by the couch, gently stroked and sometimes kissed the closed eyelids of his beautiful Diane. His left hand rested on the pillow, and his mistress's fingers, entwined in his own, clutched them from time to time as if by a convulsive movement, while her breath, at once sweet and burning, touched his lips with a voluptuous caress.

" Dearest," said he at last, " you seem to me to be suffering from something worse than headache. Has anything grieved you ? Why do you not tell me what it is ? Do you not know that love obliges us to share our pains as well as our pleasures ? "

The countess shook her head, but did not open her eyes. Her lips moved, but made no articulate sound ; and then, as if exhausted by even this effort, she let her head sink back on Mergy's shoulder. As she did so, the clock struck half-past eleven. Diane started, and sat up trembling.

" But really," said Mergy, " you terrify me, my beautiful one !"

" Nothing—nothing yet ! " said she, in a muffled tone. " How hideous that clock sounds ! At each stroke I feel as it were a red-hot iron piercing my heart ! "

Mergy could not devise any better cure, or any better answer, than to kiss her forehead as she leant it towards him. Suddenly she stretched out her hands, and laid them on her lover's shoulders ; while still half-lying back, she bent on him a gaze so glittering that it seemed as if it would pierce him through.

" Bernard," said she, " when are you going to be converted ? "

" Dear angel ! let us not talk of that to-day ; it will make you still more unwell."

" It is your stubbornness that makes me ill ; but that matters little to you. Besides, time presses ; and were I dying, I could gladly spend my last breath in exhorting you."

Mergy tried to shut her mouth with a kiss,—a very good argument of its kind, and one which serves as an answer to every possible question which can be put to a lover by his mistress. But Diane, who as a rule met him half-way on such occasions, repulsed him this time vigorously, and almost indignantly.

" Hear me, M. de Mergy ! " she cried. " Every day I weep tears of blood as I think of you and the error of your ways. You know whether I love you or not. Judge what I must suffer when I think that he who is far dearer to me

than life may, perhaps at any moment, perish body and
soul!"

"Diane, you know that we agreed never to talk on such
subjects again."

"But we *must*, unhappy man! How do you know that
you have even an hour left for repentance?"

The unusual tone of her voice and her singular expres-
sions reminded Mergy, against his will, of the strange
advice which he had just received from Béville. He could
not hinder a feeling of emotion; but he restrained himself,
and set down this excess of zeal for proselytizing to mere
religious fervour.

"What do you mean, fair love?" asked he. "Do you
think the ceiling is going to fall in order to kill a Huguenot,
as the canopy of your couch did yesterday? It was lucky
we escaped then at the expense of a little dust!"

"Your obstinacy drives me to despair!" she replied.
"Listen: I dreamt just now that your foes were making
ready to kill you; I saw you torn and bleeding in their
hands; I saw you give up the ghost before I could bring
my confessor to your side!"

"My foes? I did not know I had any."

"Madman! are not all those who hate heresy your
enemies? Is not that all France? Yes! all Frenchmen
must be your foes, so long as you are the foe of God and
His Church!"

"No more of this, my queen! As for your dreams, you
must go to old Camilla to expound them; I have no skill
in that. But let us change the subject. You have been to
Court to-day, I suppose? It must have been there you
caught this headache which tortures you and maddens me."

"Yes, Bernard, I have been at Court. I have seen the

Queen ; and I left her with my mind made up to make a last attempt at bringing about a change in you. You must — you absolutely must abjure !"

" I think," interrupted Bernard, " that since, my fair love, you are strong enough to preach so earnestly, despite your illness, we might, we really might, if you would permit it, employ our time better still."

She received the pleasantry with a glance half-scornful, half-angry.

" Hardened man !" said she in a low voice, and as if speaking to herself; " why am I so weak with him ?" Then continuing louder, " I see clearly enough that you do not love me, and I rank with you not even a little dearer than your horse. Provided I minister to your pleasure, what does it matter if I am miserable ? For you—for you alone —I have consented to suffer the torments of conscience, beside which all torments of man's invention and man's hatred are nothing. A word of your mouth would restore the peace of my soul, and this word you will not speak ! You will not sacrifice for my sake a single prejudice of your own !"

" Dear Diane, how you persecute me !" said Mergy. " Be just, and let not your zeal for your religion blind you. Answer me, will you ever find a slave more docile than I in everything that body or soul can do for you ? But if I must repeat it once more, I can die for you, but I cannot, for you, believe in certain things."

She shrugged her shoulders as she heard him speak, and she looked at him with an expression almost akin to hatred.

" I cannot," he went on, " change for you my brown locks to fair ; I cannot alter the shape of my limbs to please you. My religion is a part of me, dearest, and a part which can only

be torn from me with my life.   They might preach to me for
         twenty years, but never make me believe that a
         morsel of unleavened bread—   "

         "Silence!" interrupted she in a tone of com-
         mand.   "No blasphemies!   I have tried
         everything without effect.   You   all of you
         who are infected with the poison of
         heresy—are a people
         hardened   in   head

and heart, and you shut
your ears and eyes to
the truth lest you should
see and hear with them.
Well, the time has come when you shall
neither hear nor see.   There was but one means
left to cauterize this wound in the Church, and that means
is to be employed."

She paced the chamber with a troubled mien, and then went on :

" In less than an hour the seven heads of the dragon of heresy will be lopped off. The sword is sharpened, the faithful are ready, the infidels shall be swept from the face of the earth ! " Then, stretching her finger to the clock in the corner of the room —" See ! " she said, " you have still a quarter of an hour for repentance. When the hand reaches that figure your fate will be sealed ! "

She was still speaking, when a dull sound like to that of a crowd hovering round a mighty fire began to make itself heard, at first indistinctly ; but it seemed to grow quickly, and after a very few minutes the tolling of bells and the report of firearms were heard afar off.

" What hideous news is this ? " cried Mergy.

But the countess had darted to the window and had opened it. Then the noise, hitherto muffled by the glass and the curtains, came in more clearly. Shrieks of pain and yells of joy seemed to be distinguishable in it. A crimson smoke rose to the sky, and appeared to hang over every part of the city as far as the eye could reach. It would have seemed a vast conflagration, if a smell of resin, which could only have been produced by thousands of lighted torches, had not quickly filled the chamber. At the same time the flash of a musket which seemed to have been discharged in the street itself lit up for a moment the windows of an adjoining house.

" The massacre has begun ! " cried the countess, putting her hands in horror to her head.

" What massacre ? What do you mean ? "

" To-night all the Huguenots are to be slain by the King's orders. All Catholics are under arms, and not a heretic is to be spared. France and the Church are saved. But *you* — you are lost if you do not abjure your false belief."

Mergy felt all his limbs covered with cold sweat. He stared with haggard eyes at Diane de Turgis, whose features expressed a singular mixture of anguish and triumph. The hideous din which echoed in his ears, and filled all the town, sufficiently attested the truth of the appalling news he had just heard. For some moments the countess remained motionless, her eyes fixed speechlessly on him, her finger still stretched towards the window. She seemed to appeal to Mergy's fancy to show him the bloody scenes, as of a cannibal feast, which the howlings and torchlights suggested. By degrees her expression softened, its savage joy passed, the horror in it remained. At last, falling on her

knees, and with an imploring voice, "Bernard!" she cried, "I conjure you, save your life! Be converted! Save your life, save mine, which is bound up in yours!"

Mergy glared fiercely at her as she followed him, still on her knees and with outstretched arms, through the chamber. Answering never a word, he rushed to the end of the oratory and seized his sword, which at his entrance he had placed on a chair.

"Miserable man!" cried the countess, hastening to him, "what would you do?"

"Defend myself," he answered. "They will not kill *me* like a sheep!"

"Madman! A thousand swords could not save you. The whole town is in arms. The King's Guards, the Swiss, the citizens, the populace, all are engaged in the massacre; and not a Huguenot but has at this moment a dozen daggers at his breast. There is one only means of rescue from death. Become a Catholic!"

Mergy was a brave man; but as he thought of the dangers which the night seemed to threaten, he felt, for a moment, base fear thrilling to the bottom of his heart, and even the notion of saving himself by apostasy flashed like lightning across his mind.

"I can answer for your life if you abjure!" said Diane, clasping her hands.

"If I do so," thought he, "I shall despise myself for the rest of it." And the thought restored his courage, which was doubled by very shame at his own momentary wavering.

He crushed his hat on his head, drew his belt tight, and rolling his cloak round his left arm buckler-wise, he made a steady stride towards the door.

"Where are you going, wretch?" cried she.

"Into the street. I should not like you to have the grief of seeing me butchered under your eyes and in your house."

There was so deep a tone of contempt in his voice that the countess was overwhelmed. She had thrown herself in his way, and he repulsed her roughly enough. But she seized the skirt of his doublet, and dragged herself on her knees behind him.

"Unhand me!" he cried. "Would you deliver me yourself to the assassins' daggers? A Huguenot's mistress can ransom her sins by sacrificing her lover's blood to her Deity!"

"Stay, Bernard, I implore you! It is only your soul's health I desire. Live for me, dear angel! Save yourself in the name of our love—consent to pronounce a single word, and I swear you are safe!"

"What? I accept the faith of brigands and of murderers! Holy martyrs of the Gospel, I come to join you!"

And he tore himself so fiercely from her that the countess fell sharply on the floor. He was about to open the door and depart, when Diane, rising with the agility of a tigress, sprang upon him and clasped him in her arms with a grip stronger than that of a strong man.

"Bernard!" she cried in a transport, and with streaming eyes, "I love you more than if you had abjured!" and dragging him to the couch, she flung herself and him upon it, and covered him with kisses and with tears.

"Stay here, my only love! Stay with me, my brave Bernard!" she said, hugging him, and twining her body round him like a serpent enlacing its prey. "They will not seek you here : not in my arms : and did they so, they must kill me to reach your breast ! Pardon me, dear love ! I could not warn you sooner of the danger which threatened : I was bound by a terrible oath, but I will save you now or perish with you !"

At this moment a loud knock at the street gate was heard. The countess uttered a piercing shriek, and Mergy, disengaging himself from her embrace, with his cloak still wrapped round his left arm, felt so full of strength and resolution, that he would have plunged headlong on a band of a hundred assassins if they had showed themselves.

In the entrance gate of almost all Parisian houses there was a small wicket, closely barred with iron, so that the inmates could reconnoitre beforehand whether it was safe for them to open. Sometimes even heavy oaken gates, strengthened with nails and bands of iron, were not enough to reassure careful folk, who did not want to surrender before they were regularly besieged. Narrow loopholes were therefore worked at each side of the gate, and from these, without being seen, they could comfortably rake the assailants. An old confidential equerry of the countess, after examining the person who had presented himself through some such a barred wicket, and after duly interrogating him, came back and told his mistress that Captain George de Mergy pressed for instant admittance. All fear thus passed away, and the gate was opened.

CHAPTER XXII.

THE
TWENTY-FOURTH OF
AUGUST.

"Bleed them! bleed them!"
*(Words of the Marshal
de Tavannes.)*

AFTER leaving his squadron,
Captain George hastened home,
hoping to find his brother there; but he
had already gone out, telling his servant
that he should be away all night. George
had had no difficulty in guessing
that he was with the

countess, and had made all haste to seek him there.
But the massacre had already begun; and the tumult, the
throng of butchers, and the chains stretched across the
streets, checked him at every step. He was obliged to
pass by the Louvre, and there fanaticism showed its mad-
ness to the full. Many Protestants inhabited the quarter,
which was now invaded by the Papist citizens and the
soldiers of the Guards, sword and torch in hand. There,
according to the striking expression of a contemporary
writer, "blood ran in all directions, seeking its way to the
river,"[1] and it was impossible to pass along the streets
without risk of being crushed at every minute by corpses
flung from the windows. By a devilish precaution, most
of the boats, which as a rule were moored along the Louvre
front, had been taken across the stream; so that many
fugitives who ran to the Seine bank, hoping there to take
boat and escape from their enemies' blows, found no more
choice but betwixt the water and the halberds of the soldiers
who chased them. Meanwhile, at one of the palace
windows, men saw, it is said, Charles IX., armed with a
long arquebuss, and "potting like game"[2] the unfortunate
passers-by.

The captain, striding over dead bodies and splashing
himself with their blood, made good his way, at the risk,
every moment, of being sacrificed to some assassin's mistake.
He had noticed that every soldier and armed citizen wore
a white scarf on his arm and a white cross in his hat. He
might easily have adopted the badge; but his horror of
the murderers extended even to the signs by which they
recognized each other. On the river bank, near the

[1] D'Aubigné, "Histoire Universelle."
[2] *Ibid.* ["Qui giboyait." *Translator.*]

Châtelet, he heard his name called ; he turned his head, and saw a man who, armed to the teeth, but apparently making no use of his weapons, wore the white cross in his hat, and was twisting a scrap of paper in his fingers with a wholly unconcerned air. It was Béville, placidly gazing at the bodies, dead and alive, which were being flung into the Seine from the Miller's Bridge.

"What the devil are you doing here, George?" said he. "Is it a miracle? or is it special grace which inspires you with this holy zeal? for you look as if you had joined the Huguenot hunt."

"What are you doing yourself amid these wretches?" answered George.

"I? I am looking on. By Jove! it is something to see. And do you know, I have done a good stroke of business. You know old Michael Cornabon, the Huguenot money-lender, who has plucked me so clean?"

"Wretch! have you killed him?"

"I? fie on you! I have nothing to do with religious affairs. So far from killing him, I have hidden him in my cellar, and for his part he has given me a receipt in full for all I owe him. Thus I have both done a noble deed and have been rewarded therefor. It is true that, in order to make him sign the receipt more easily, I had to hold a pistol twice to his head ; but may the devil take me if I meant to pull the trigger. Ah! now : look at that woman who has caught by her skirts on one of the bridge beams. She will fall—no she won't! Plague on it, that is a curious sight, and deserves to be looked at closer."

George left him, and as he did so, struck his forehead, crying, "And to think that that is one of the honestest gentlemen I know in this town to-night!"

He now set foot in the Rue St. Josse, which was deserted and dark : clearly none of the dwellers there were Protestants. Yet the noise from the neighbouring streets was quite distinctly heard, and suddenly the ruddy glow of torches lit up the white walls. He heard piercing cries, and saw a woman, who fled with superhuman speed, half naked, with dishevelled hair, and holding a child in her arms. Pursuing her were two men, cheering each other on with savage cries, like huntsmen after a wild beast. She was just about to rush into an open passage, when one of her pursuers fired an arquebuss, with which he was armed, at her. The shot struck her in the back, and brought her down : but she rose quickly, made one step towards George, and fell once more on her knees. Then, with a supreme effort, she lifted her child towards the captain, as though relying on his generosity, and died without a word.

"Another heretic baggage down!" cried the marksman ; " I will not rest till I have made up the dozen !"

" Wretch !" cried the captain, and he fired a pistol point-blank at him. The scoundrel's head struck the wall hard by, his eyes gave one terrible glare, and his heels slipping from beneath him, he fell like a log of wood with its support struck away, plump and stone-dead on the ground.

" What ! kill a Catholic !" cried his companion, who held a torch in one hand, and a bloody sword in the other. " Who are you ? By the mass ! you are one of the King's light horse ! Good sir, you mistake !"

The captain drew a second pistol from his belt, and cocked it. The motion and the click were perfectly understood, and the murderer, dropping his torch, fled at full speed. George, not condescending to fire after him, stooped, examined the woman who was stretched on the ground, and saw that she was dead. The ball had pierced her through and through; but her child, whose arms clasped his mother's neck, wailed and wept: he was covered with blood, but he had miraculously escaped a wound. With some difficulty the captain tore him from his mother, to whom the child clung with all his strength, and wrapped him up in his own cloak. Then, taking warning by the recent brush, he picked up the dead man's hat, and taking the white cross out of it placed it on his own. In which fashion he made his way without further hindrance to the countess's house.

The two brothers fell into each other's arms, and for some time remained in this embrace without speaking. At last the captain in few words described the state of the town. Bernard, cursing the King, the Guises, and the priests, expressed his anxiety to go forth and to seek to join his brethren in the faith, on the chance that they might somewhere try to make head against their enemies. The countess wept

K K

and held him back ; while the child cried and asked for
his mother.

After spending a considerable time in exclamations,
groans, and tears, they felt it necessary to fix on some
course of action. As for the child, the countess's equerry
undertook the business of finding a woman to take charge
of him. It was impossible for Mergy to depart at such a
moment ; and besides, where was he to go ? and how did
anyone know whether or no the massacre was spreading
all over France ? Strong parties had certainly occupied the
bridges over which the Protestants might have passed into
the Faubourg St. Germain, and thence have escaped from
the town and gained the southern provinces, always inclined
to their cause. On the other hand, to ask the King's mercy
at a moment when, in the heat of slaughter, he thought of
nothing but new victims, seemed doubtfully wise, and even
certainly foolish. The countess's house, thanks to her
repute for devotion, was not likely to be narrowly searched
by the murderers ; and Diane thought she might answer
for her own people. So Mergy could not fix on any
place of retreat where he ran less risk, and it was decided
that he should hide himself there and see what would
happen.

Daylight, so far from putting a stop to the massacres,
seemed only to increase them and make them more business-
like. Every Catholic, under penalty of being suspected of
heresy, had to mount the white cross, and either take arms
or denounce such Huguenots as were still living. The
King, shutting himself up in his palace, gave access to no
one but the chiefs of the murderers ; the populace, induced
by hope of pillage, had joined the trained bands and the
soldiers ; while preachers in the churches exhorted the

faithful to redoubled excesses of cruelty. "Let us,' said they, "once for all crush the hydra's heads, and for ever put an end to civil war!" And, in order to persuade the bloodthirsty and miracle-craving mob that heaven approved its rage and had encouraged it by a striking prodigy, "Go," cried they, "to the Cemetery of the Innocents; go and see the hawthorn which has just blossomed a second time with a new and vigorous youth as having been watered with heretic blood!"

Numerous processions of armed murderers marched with all ceremony to worship the Holy Thorn, and left the cemetery flushed with fresh zeal to discover and slay those whom heaven thus clearly sentenced. A saying of Catherine's was in every mouth, and was repeated by those who were butchering women and children: "*Che pietà lor ser crudele, che crudeltà lor ser pietoso*"—"To-day there is mercy in being cruel; there is cruelty in being merciful."

Strange to say, though there were few among all these Protestants who had not seen war—who had not taken part in desperate battles, where they had endeavoured, and often successfully, to make valour atone for want of numbers—yet during this butchery two only attempted any resistance to their murderers. Of these two, one only was a soldier. It may be that the habit of fighting in bodies, and after a regular fashion, had robbed them of the individual energy which might have prompted each Huguenot to defend himself in his house as in a castle. But old warriors were seen, like victims devoted to sacrifice, holding out their throats to rascals who, the day before, would have trembled before them—taking, as it were, resignation for courage, and preferring the renown of martyrs to a soldier's honourable death.

When the first thirst of blood was quenched, the more merciful of the butchers commonly offered life to their victims at the price of abjuration; but a very small number of Calvinists availed themselves of the offer, and consented to ransom themselves from death and torture by a perhaps excusable falsehood. Even women and children repeated their confession of faith beneath the drawn swords and died without a murmur.

After two days of such slaughter the King tried to stop it; but when the reins have been thrown on the neck of popular passions, it is impossible to check them. Not only did the daggers continue active, but the King himself, accused of unorthodox compassion, was obliged to withdraw his suggestion of mercy, and even to exaggerate the malevolence which at all times was more or less natural to his character.

During the first few days after the St. Bartholomew Mergy was regularly visited in his hiding-place by his brother, who gave him each time fresh particulars of the horrible scenes he had witnessed.

"Ah! when shall I be able to quit this country of crime and murder?" cried George. "I would rather live among wild beasts than among Frenchmen."

"Come with me to La Rochelle," said Mergy; "I have good hope that the assassins have not won it yet. Come and die with me, obliterating your apostasy by defending the last bulwark of our faith."

"Ah! and what is to become of *me?*" Diane would cry.

"Then let us go to Germany or England," answered George. "There, at any rate, we need be neither murdered nor murderers."

But nothing came of these schemes. George was thrown into prison for disobedience to the King's orders; and the countess, in terror lest her lover should be discovered, had no thought but how to get him out of Paris.

CHAPTER XXIII.

THE TWO MONKS.

*" And thus they made of him a monk
By putting a cowl upon him."*
Folk-Song.

IN a tavern on the banks of the Loire, not far from Orleans, as you go down towards Beaugency, a young monk, in a brown robe with a large hood half-drawn over his face, was seated before a

*" Lui mettant un Capuchon
Ils en firent un moine."*
Chanson Populaire. *[Translator's Note.]*

table, his eyes fixed on his breviary with the most edifying
attention, though the corner which he had chosen was a
little dark for reading in. He had at his girdle a rosary,
the beads of which were rather larger than pigeons' eggs,
while an abundant supply of medals, with the effigies of
saints, were hung to the same girdle, and clinked at every
movement that he made. When he lifted his head to look
in the direction of the door, there might have been seen a
very well-shaped mouth, adorned with a moustache twisted
into the shape of a Turkish bow, and modish enough to
do credit to a captain of gendarmes. His hands were very
white, his nails long and carefully trimmed ; nor was there
any sign to show that the young brother had ever, as by
the rule of his order he should have done, wielded a spade
or a rake.

A plump and chubby-cheeked peasant woman, who
doubled the parts of waitress and cook in the tavern, being
also the mistress herself, drew near the young monk, and
curtseying awkwardly, said :

"Well, father, are you going to order something for your
dinner ? Do you know that it is past noon ?"

"Will the Beaugency boat be long before it is here ?"
answered he.

"Who knows ?" said she. "The water is low, and they
cannot take their own time. Besides, anyhow, it is not due
yet. I should dine here if I were you."

"So I will : but have you no other room than this to eat
in ? There is a smell here that I do not like."

"You are very particular, father. I cannot smell anything at all."

"Then are you singeing pigs close to the inn ?"

"Pigs ? Ha ! ha ! That is funny. Pigs ? Yes ; or

something like it. They *are* pigs in their way, for, as the
saying is, they were dressed in silk[1] in their lifetime ; but
they are not pigs good to eat. These, saving your reverence,
father, are Huguenots whom they are burning on the river
bank, some hundred yards off, and it is the scent of them
that you perceive."

"Huguenots ?"

"Yes, Huguenots. Do you mind that ? It need not
take away your appetite. And as for changing your dining-
room, I have no other ; so you must make the best of this.
Ah ! the smell of roasted Huguenot is not so bad ! Besides,
if they were not burnt they might smell worse. There was
a heap of them on the bank this morning—a heap as high
as our chimney-piece !"

"And do you go and look at these corpses ?"

"Ah, you mean because they were naked ? Dead men
do not count, holy father ; I did not think any more of them
than if I had seen a heap of dead frogs. But all the same,
they must have done a fine business at Orleans yesterday,
for the Loire has brought us shoals of these heretic fish ;
and as the river is low they are found high and dry on the
shingle every day. Why yesterday, when our miller's man
looked to see how many tench were in his net, look you,
there was a dead woman in it, with a halberd wound right in
the middle of her ! It went in at her waist and came out at
her shoulders. Marry, but he would rather have found a
fine carp though ! But what is the matter with your reverence ? Are you going to swoon ? Shall I fill you a cup
of Beaugency wine while you wait for your dinner ? That
will set you right inside."

---

[1] [A play, not by any device to be kept in English, between *soie* "silk,"
and *soie* "pig's bristle."]—*Translator's Note.*

"Thank you, no."

"Well then, what will you have for dinner?"

"Whatever comes to hand—I care little."

"Yes; but what? My larder is well furnished, look you!"

"Well then, give me a

chicken, and leave me to read my breviary."

"A chicken! your reverence. A chicken! that is a pretty thing! The spiders need not look to weave their webs over *your* teeth on fast days. Have you got a dispensation from the Pope to eat chickens on Friday?"

"Bah! how absent-minded I am!" said he. "Of course, to-day is Friday. 'On Friday thou shalt not eat flesh.' Give me some eggs, and take my best thanks for reminding me in time to prevent so great a sin."

"Look you now," said the hostess half to herself, "these

gentry will eat chickens on a fast day if you do not remind them, and yet will make a fuss to make your blood run cold if they find a morsel of bacon in poor folks' broth!" Which said, she set to work to cook her eggs, and the monk returned to his breviary.

"Ave Maria! my sister," said another monk, who entered the tavern at the very moment that Dame Marguerite, frying-pan handle in hand, was about to turn an omelet of large dimensions.

The newcomer was a handsome old man, grey-bearded, tall, strongly made, and stout. His face was very highly complexioned; but its most remarkable feature was a huge patch, which hid one eye and half covered the cheek. He spoke French glibly enough, but with a slight though noticeable foreign accent.

As he came in the younger monk drew his hood still closer, so that his face could not be seen; but Dame Marguerite was even more surprised to perceive that the last comer, who had thrown his hood back because of the heat, pulled it on the moment that he had spied his brother in orders.

"Faith, father," said the hostess, "you have come in the nick of time for dinner. You will not have to wait, and you will find yourself among friends." Then turning to the younger monk, "You will be delighted, your reverence, will you not, to dine with his reverence here? The smell of my omelet has brought him, and no wonder, for by Our Lady I do not spare butter."

The young monk replied shyly and stammering, "I am afraid I shall be in the gentleman's way:" while the elder, stooping his head still lower, answered, "I am a poor monk of Alsace; I speak French badly, and I fear my company will not please my brother."

"Come, come!" cried Dame Marguerite; "how polite you both are! Monks, and monks of the same order, ought to have but one board and one bed," and she thrust a stool up to the table, right opposite the young friar. The elder seated himself, apparently much embarrassed, and struggling between hunger and a certain dislike to face his colleague. She dished the omelet, and said, "Now, good fathers, be quick with your grace, and then tell me whether my omelet is good."

But the mere word "grace" seemed to put the two monks still less at their ease. The younger said to the elder, "It is for you to say grace. You are my senior, and the honour is yours."

"Nay," quoth he, "not at all. You were here before me, and you have the right to say it."

"I pray you set me the example."

"I could not think of doing so."

"But really you must."

"Look at them," said Dame Marguerite; "they will let my omelet get cold! Did anyone ever see two of Saint Francis's children so scrupulous? Let the old one bless the meat, and the young one shall give thanks afterwards."

"I can only say grace in my own tongue," said the old monk. The younger looked much surprised, and stole a glance at his companion. He, however, clasping his hands most devoutly, began to mutter in his hood certain words which conveyed no meaning to anyone, then he sat down, and, without another word, he had in no time devoured three parts of the omelet and drained the bottle set before him. His fellow, with his nose in his plate, never opened his mouth, save to eat; and when the omelet was finished he rose, clasped his hands, and uttered hastily, slurring them over, certain Latin words, the last of which were *et beata viscera virginis Mariæ.* Marguerite heard these last, and these only.

"What a queer grace (with reverence be it spoken) you said then, father? It is not like those that our curé says."

"That is the grace used in our convent," said the young Franciscan.

"Will the boat soon come?" said the elder.

"Patience!" answered Dame Marguerite; "it is not nearly here yet."

The younger monk seemed to be vexed, as far as could be judged by a twitch of his head. But he did not make the slightest remark; and taking up his breviary, began to read it with increased attention. The Alsatian, on his part, turned his back to his companion, and began to pass the beads of his rosary between his finger and thumb, moving his lips, but without producing the least sound from them.

"These are the strangest and most silent monks that

ever I saw," thought Dame Marguerite, sitting down to her
wheel, which she soon set going.

No sound save the whirring of the wheel had broken the
silence for a good quarter of an hour, when four ill-looking
fellows, well armed, entered the inn. They touched their
hats slightly at sight of the monks, and one of them, addressing Marguerite familiarly as "my little Meg," bade her give
them wine at once and dinner soon. "For," said he, "the
moss is growing in my throat, so long is it since my jaws
were in motion."

"Wine? wine?" grumbled Marguerite; "that is easily
said, Master Bois-Dauphin, but are you going to pay the
shot? Jack Trust-Me is dead, you know; and besides, you
owe me already, for wine, dinners, and suppers, six crowns
and more, as I am an honest woman."

"The one thing is as true as the other," said Bois-Dauphin laughing; "that is to say, Mother Meg, I owe you two
crowns, and not a penny more." His actual words were
somewhat stronger than these.

"Oh Jesus! oh Mary! how can you say so?"

"Come, come, no noise, old lady. Let it be six crowns, if
you like. I will pay you, Maggie, and our score to-day as
well, for I have the chinks in my pocket, though this present
business is a scurvy one for profit. I cannot think what
the rascals do with their money."

"Perhaps they swallow it, like the Germans," said one of
his comrades.

"A plague!" cried Bois-Dauphin; "we must look to that.
Good coins in a heretic carcass are a good joke, but not one
that ought to be thrown to the dogs."

"How the minister's daughter shrieked this morning,"
said the third fellow.

" Yes ! and the fat parson too ! " added the fourth. " How I did laugh at him ! he was so fat he would not sink."

" Then you worked hard to-day ? " said Marguerite, coming back from the cellar with her bottles full.

" Pretty fair," said Bois-Dauphin. "What with men, women, and children, we made up a dozen, thrown into the water or into the fire. But the worst of it was, Maggie, that they had not a rap : except the woman, who had some trinkets, the whole bag was not worth a hound's four shoes. Yes, father," added he, addressing the younger monk, " we earned plenty of indulgences this morning by killing your enemies, the dog heretics."

The monk gazed at him a moment, and then returned to his reading : but his breviary quivered in his left hand, and his right was clenched like that of a man in strong emotion.

" And talking of indulgences," said Bois-Dauphin, turning to his comrades, " do you know I should like one to eat meat to-day ? There are some chickens in our dame's poultry-yard which are desperately tempting."

" Let us eat them," said one of the wretches ; " we shall not be damned for that. We will go to confession to-morrow, and that will make it right."

" Listen, brothers," said another ; " I have an idea ; let us ask these plump frocked gentry here to give us a licence for meat."

" As if they could ! " said his comrade.

" By Our Lady's body ! " cried Bois-Dauphin, "I know a better way than that, and I'll whisper it to you."

The four rascals laid their heads together, and Bois-Dauphin explained to them, in an undertone, his plan, which was received with shouts of laughter. But one of the bravoes seemed to hesitate.

"That is an ill device of yours, Bois-Dauphin," said he, "and it may bring us bad luck. I will not make one."

"Hold your tongue, Guillemain! 'Tis a mighty sin, forsooth, to make a man smell the blade of a dagger."

"Yes; but a shaveling!"

They were conversing in a low tone, and the two monks seemed to be trying to guess their topic of conversation by the words caught here and there.

"Bah! it makes no difference," replied Bois-Dauphin speaking a little louder; "and besides, in this way the sin will lie on him and not on me."

"Yes, yes! Bois-Dauphin is right," cried the other. So he rose at once and left the room. A moment later the poultry were heard making a noise, and the ruffian soon reappeared with a dead chicken in each hand.

"Ah! son of perdition!" cried Dame Marguerite; "kill my chickens, and on Friday too? What are you going to do with them, wretch?"

"Hold your tongue, Dame Maggie, and don't make my ears burn. You know that I am an ugly customer. Get your spits ready and leave me alone." Then, drawing near to the Alsatian friar, he said, "Now, father, you see these two animals? I want you to be so good as to christen them."

The monk started back with surprise; his reverend brother closed his book, and Dame Marguerite showered strong language on Bois-Dauphin.

"You want me to christen them?" said the monk.

"Yes, my father. I will be their godfather, Meg here shall be godmother; and these are the names that I give my godchildren; this shall be called Carp, and this Perch. There be two very pretty names."

"Christen chickens?" cried the monk with a laugh.

" Yes, father. Come, set to work."

" Wretch!" cried Marguerite, "do you think I will allow such work as this in my house? Do you think you are among Jews, or at a witch's sabbath, that you christen beasts?"

" Take this chatterbox off me," said Bois-Dauphin to his fellows; "and as for you, father, perhaps you could read the name of the cutler who forged this blade?"

As he spoke he passed his bare poniard under the old monk's nose. The younger half rose on his bench, but almost immediately, as though after discreet reflection, he sat down again, determined to abide patiently.

" But how am I to baptize poultry, my son?" said the elder.

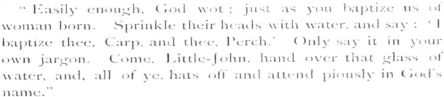

" Easily enough, God wot; just as you baptize us of woman born. Sprinkle their heads with water, and say : ' I baptize thee, Carp, and thee, Perch.' Only say it in your own jargon. Come, Little-John, hand over that glass of water, and, all of ye, hats off and attend piously in God's name."

To the general surprise the old cordelier took some water, shed it on the fowls' heads, and pronouncing very rapidly and very indistinctly something which sounded like a prayer, ended with *baptizo te Carpam et Percham.* Then he sat down again, and told his beads once more with great tranquillity, as if he had done something quite in the common way. Dame Marguerite stood dumb with amazement ; but Bois-Dauphin was in his glory. "Come, Meg !" said he, throwing the chickens to her, " dress us this carp and this perch. They will make a capital fast-day dinner." But notwithstanding the baptism, Dame Marguerite still refused to consider them fit food for Christians, and the ruffians had to threaten her with personal violence before she could make up her mind to spit the improvised fishes.

Bois-Dauphin and his companions meanwhile drank copiously, toasting healths, and making a great clatter.

" Listen," said Bois-Dauphin at last, smiting the table hard to enjoin silence. " I am going to drink a health to our Holy Father the Pope, and death to all Huguenots. These two cowled gentry and Dame Marget shall join us."

The suggestion was received by his comrades with applause, and he rose, staggering somewhat (for he was more than half drunk already), and filled the young monk's glass from the bottle in his hand.

" Come, good father," said he, " to the Holiness of his health ! Bah ! a slip of the tongue. To the health of his Holiness, and to the death———"

" I never drink between meals," said the young man coolly.

" Ah ! but you shall drink now, devil take me ! or tell the reason why."

So speaking, he set the bottle on the table, and seizing the glass, held it to the lips of the monk, who was leaning over his breviary in great apparent calm. Some drops of wine fell on the book. Then the monk rose, clutched the glass, and instead of drinking it, flung its contents full in Bois-Dauphin's face.

The company roared with laughter; and the monk, his back to the wall, and his arms crossed, gazed at the ruffian.

" Do you know, little father, that I do not like that joke? By God! if you were not a monk, I would pay you, by teaching you to know with whom you are dealing." And as he spoke, he thrust his hand close to the young man's face, and just twitched his moustache with his finger ends.

Then the monk's countenance flamed scarlet. With one hand he collared the insolent scoundrel, and with the other he grasped the bottle, and smashed it on Bois-Dauphin's head with such force that he fell senseless on the floor, drenched at once with wine and blood.

" Well done, my boy!" cried the old monk. " You have a heavy hand for one of the cloth!"

" Bois-Dauphin is killed!" cried the three assassins, seeing that their comrade did not stir. " Scoundrel! We will curry your hide for you!" and they grasped their swords. But the young monk, with surprising alertness, tucked up the long sleeves of his gown, got possession of Bois-Dauphin's sword, and threw himself into a posture of defence, in the most resolute way in the world. At the same moment, his brother monk drew from beneath his cassock a dagger, with a blade half-a-yard long, and took position by the other's side, with an air not less soldierly. " Now, blackguards!" cried he, " we will teach you how to behave, and give you a lesson in your own business." And in the twinkling of an eye the three scoundrels, wounded or disarmed, were driven to jump through the window.

" Jesu Maria!" cried Dame Marguerite, " you are stout men-at-arms, holy fathers! You do religion credit! Still there is a man killed, and that is awkward for my house's reputation."

" Not a bit of it," said the old monk. " He is not killed, I see him wriggling. But I will give him extreme unction." Then, drawing near the wounded man, he caught him by his hair, set the edge of the dagger to his throat, and would have cut his head off, if Dame Marguerite and his fellow monk had not stopped him.

" Good God!" said Marguerite, " what are you doing ? Kill a man ? And a man who passes for a good Catholic ? — though, as you have seen, he is nothing of the kind."

" I guess," said the young monk to his brother, " that urgent business calls you, as it does me, to Beaugency. There is the boat ; let us lose no time."

" You are right ; I am with you," said he : and wiping his dagger, he replaced it under his gown. Then the two valiant monks, after paying their score, went side by side to the Loire, leaving Bois-Dauphin in Marguerite's hands. She began by rummaging his pockets, and paying herself : then she set to work to pick out the bits of glass with which his face bristled, and to dress his wounds according to the regular fashion of good women in such cases.

" Unless I am much mistaken, I have seen you somewhere," said the young man to the old Franciscan.

" And may the devil take me if I do not know your face too. But——"

" When I saw you first, I do not think you wore that cassock."

" And how about yourself ? "

" Then you are Captain——"

" Dietrich Hornstein, at your service. And you are the gentleman with whom I dined once near Étampes ? "

" I am."

" Then your name is Mergy ? "

" It is : but not just now. I am Friar Ambrose."

" And I am Friar Anthony of Alsace."

" Very well. And where are you going ? "

" To La Rochelle, if I can get there."

" So am I."

" I am charmed to meet you. But, the devil! you put me in a desperate fix with your 'grace'! I did not know a word of it ; and I took you for a real monk if ever there was one."

" I can return the compliment."

" But where did you escape from ? " said Hornstein.

" From Paris. And you ? "

" From Orleans : I had to hide for more than a week. My poor troopers, cornet and all, are in the Loire."

" And Mila ? "

" She turned Catholic."

" And my horse, captain ? "

" Ah : your horse? Well, I made the rascal trumpeter who robbed you run the gauntlet. But as I did not know where you lived, I could not send the horse back ; and so you see I kept him till I should have the honour of meeting you. Now, no doubt, he belongs to some scoundrelly Papist."

" Hush, captain ! Do not say that word so loud. But come, let us join our fortunes together, and be allies as we were just now."

" So be it : as long as Dietrich Hornstein has a drop of blood in his veins he will be ready to play a good knife at your side." And they struck hands thereon joyfully.

" But now I think on it, tell me what they meant with

their chickens and their *Carpam, Percham?* Truly these
Papists are a pack of idiots."

"Hush, again! here is the boat."

Talking thus, they came to the vessel, went on board, and
reached Beaugency without farther accident, except meeting
divers corpses of their brethren in the faith floating on the
Loire.

One of the boatmen observed that most of these corpses
floated face upwards. "They are imploring vengeance
from heaven!" whispered Mergy to the captain of Reiters,
and Dietrich squeezed his hand in answer.

CHAPTER XXIV.

THE SIEGE OF LA ROCHELLE.

"Still hope and suffer all who can!"
MOORE, *The Fudge Family.*

L A ROCHELLE, almost the entire population of which professed the Reformed Faith, was at this time a kind of capital to the provinces of the south, and the staunchest bulwark of the Protestant party. Extensive commercial relations with Spain and England had brought to the town considerable wealth, and the spirit of independence which wealth begets and fosters. The inhabitants, fishers or sailors by trade, not uncommonly privateersmen, accustomed from their earliest years to the hazards of

an adventurous life, were imbued with an energy which
stood them in stead of discipline and practice in regular war.
Therefore, when the news of the massacre of the 24th of
August came, the men of Rochelle were far from giving
themselves up to the stolid resignation which, seizing upon
most Protestants, had made them despair of their cause;
but were, on the contrary, inflamed with that active and
formidable courage which despair sometimes supplies.
With one accord they made up their minds to stand the
last extremities, rather than open their gates to an enemy
who had just given so striking a proof of perfidious
savagery. While the ministers fed the flames of this zeal
by fanatical preachings, women, children, and old men
vied with each other in working at the repair of the old
fortifications and the construction of new ones. Pro-
visions and arms were collected; boats and ships were
put in commission; in short, not a moment was lost in
getting into order all the means of defence which the city
possessed. Many gentlemen who had escaped the massacres came to join the Rochellese, and inspired the most
timid with courage by the picture which they drew of the
atrocities of Saint Bartholomew. To men who had just
escaped a seemingly certain death the chances of ordinary
war were like a capful of wind to sailors who have just
weathered a hurricane. Mergy and his companion were
among the number of the fugitives who thus came to swell
the garrison of La Rochelle.

The Court of Paris, alarmed by these preparations,
regretted that it had not anticipated them, and the Marshal
de Biron approached Rochelle bearing proposals for an
understanding. The King had some ground for hoping
that his choice of Biron would please the Rochellese; for

the marshal had not only taken no part in the massacre of
Saint Bartholomew, but had saved several distinguished
Protestants, and had even levelled the guns
of the Arsenal, where he commanded, at
assassins bearing the royal cognizance. His
only demand was to be received into the
town and acknowledged there as the King's
governor, with a promise to respect all the
rights and privileges of the inhabitants, and

to leave them   the free exercise of their   religion. But
how was it possible   again to put faith
in Charles IX.'s   promises after the
slaughter of sixty thousand Protestants? Besides, during
the very course of the negotiations, the massacres continued
at Bordeaux, Biron's soldiery plundered the territory of
Rochelle, and a royal fleet seized merchant ships and
blockaded the port.

N N

The Rochellese refused admission to Biron, and answered that they could not negotiate with the King so long as he remained the Guises' prisoner: perhaps because they really believed that this family were the sole authors of the woes of Calvinism, perhaps because by a fiction, often repeated since, they wished to set at ease the consciences of those who might otherwise have held that loyalty to the King ought to have the precedence over sectarian interests. Thenceforward an understanding became impossible. Yet the King bethought him of another agent, and sent La Noue.

La Noue, surnamed Iron-arm, because of an artificial arm with which he had replaced one lost in battle, was a zealous Calvinist, who in the late civil wars had shown the utmost courage and great military skill. The Admiral, whose friend he was, had had no more able and no more faithful lieutenant. At the time of the massacre he was in the Netherlands organizing the irregular bands of insurgent Flemings against the Spanish forces. Ill-served by fortune, he had been obliged to yield himself prisoner to the Duke of Alva, by whom he had been kindly treated. Later, and when the vast effusion of blood had excited some remorse, Charles IX. demanded him from the Spaniards, and, contrary to expectation, gave him a most flattering reception. The King, always in extremes, heaped favours on one Protestant just after he had caused the murder of scores of thousands. Indeed, La Noue's fate seemed to be under some special Providence, for he had already been made prisoner twice during the third civil war, once at Jarnac and once at Montcontour, and had on each occasion been set free without ransom by the King's brother,[1] against the repre-

---

[1] The Duke of Anjou, afterwards Henri III.

sentations of many of his officers, who urged him to make
an example of a man too dangerous to be spared and too
honest to be corrupted. Charles thought that La Noue
would be mindful of his clemency, and entrusted him with
the task of exhorting the Rochellese to submit. La Noue
accepted the commission (stipulating, however, that the
King should not demand of him anything dishonourable),
and set out accompanied by an Italian priest, whose duty
was to keep an eye on his conduct.

From the very first he had the mortification of finding
that he was not trusted. He could not gain admission to
La Rochelle ; but a village in the neighbourhood was desig-
nated as a place of conference, and here, at Tadon, he met
the deputies of the city. He knew them all as a man knows
his old brethren in arms : but when he appeared not a man
held out the hand of friendship to him, not a man appeared
even to know who he was. He had to announce himself,
and then set forth the King's proposals, the substance of his
speech being, " Trust the King's promises ; for civil war is
the worst of evils." But the Mayor of La Rochelle answered,
with a bitter smile, " We see before us a man who is like
La Noue, but La Noue would not have suggested that his
brethren should submit to assassins. La Noue loved our
late lord the Admiral, and would have been bent on
avenging him rather than on bargaining with his murderers. No ; *you* are not La Noue !" The unlucky ambas-
sador, cut to the heart by these reproaches, recalled the
services which he had done to the Calvinist cause, showed
his maimed arm, and protested his devotion to religion.
Little by little the mistrust of the Rochellese melted ; they
opened their gates to La Noue, they showed him what
means of defence they had, and even urged him to put

himself at their head. The offer was very tempting to an
old soldier, and his oath to Charles included a qualification
which might be conscientiously construed in different ways.
La Noue thought that by putting himself at the head of the
Rochellese he should be in better case to bring them back
to peaceful sentiments; and he also thought that he might
reconcile the allegiance he had sworn to his King with that
which he owed to his religion. But he deceived himself.
The royal troops came to attack Rochelle; La Noue headed
every sortie, and killed plenty of Catholics. Then, returning to the city, he exhorted the townsmen to come to terms.
The result was that the Catholics vowed he had broken his
word to the King, and the Protestants accused him of
wishing to betray them.

In this plight La Noue, with every kind of disgust heaped
upon him, tried to put an end to it by exposing his life
twenty times a day.

CHAPTER XXV.

LA NOUE.

"Faneste. Cap de you! Cet homme ne se mouche pas du talon."
D'AUBIGNÉ, *Le Baron de Faneste.*

THE besieged had just made a successful sally against
the advanced works of the Catholic army. They had
filled up many yards of trench, overset divers gabions, and
killed some hundred men or so, and the detachment which
had gained this success was returning into town by the
Tadon gate. First marched Captain Dietrich and a company of arquebusiers, all with heated countenances, panting

breath, and loudly calling for drink, which showed that they had not spared themselves in the fight. Then came a numerous troop of townsmen, among whom were to be noticed more than one woman, who seemed to have borne a share in the battle. These were followed by some two score prisoners, most of them covered with wounds, and guarded by a double file of soldiers, who had much ado to defend them from the rage of the people as they passed. The rearguard was formed by some twenty mounted men, with La Noue, to whom Mergy acted as aide-de-camp, last of all. His cuirass was indented by a bullet, and his horse was wounded in two places. In his left hand he held a just-discharged pistol, and he managed his horse by the aid of a hook which issued, in place of a hand, from his right arm-piece.

"Let the prisoners pass, good friends!" he cried every instant. "Be merciful, good Rochellese! They are wounded; they are defenceless; they are enemies no longer!"

But the mob answered by fierce cries of "To the gibbet with the Papists! to the gallows with them! and long live La Noue!" Mergy and the horsemen, with some well-timed blows of their lance-butts, emphasized the generous recommendations of their leader, and the prisoners were at last conducted to the city gaol and installed, under a strong guard, in a place where they had nothing to fear from popular fury. The detachment dispersed; and La Noue, with no other following save a few gentlemen, dismounted before the townhall at the same time that the mayor came forth, followed by some citizens and an old minister of the name of Laplace.

"Well, brave La Noue," said the mayor, holding out his hand, "you have just shown these cut-throats that all brave men did not die with the Admiral!"

" The affair went fortunately enough, sir," said La Noue modestly : " we lost but five killed and few wounded."

" As it was you who led the sally, M. de la Noue," returned the mayor, " we were sure of victory beforehand."

" And what could La Noue do without the help of God ? " cried the old minister sourly. " It is the mighty God who has fought for us to-day : He has heard our prayers ! "

" It is God," said La Noue in his calm voice, " who gives victory and withholds it as He wills ; and Him only must we thank for success in war." Then turning to the mayor, " Well, Master Mayor, has the council deliberated on his Majesty's last offers ? "

" It has," answered the mayor. " We have just sent the trumpeter back to Monsieur, begging him to spare himself the trouble of summoning us afresh to surrender. Henceforward we shall answer only with musket-shots."

" Ye should have hanged the trumpeter," remarked the minister. " For is it not written, ' There be men of Belial come out of the midst of you who have striven to seduce the men of their city. . . . But thou shalt not spare to slay them ; thy hand shall be first on them, and then the hand of all the people ' ? "

La Noue sighed and looked to heaven, but made no answer.

" What ! " continued the mayor, " surrender ? Surrender, when the walls are standing ? when the foe does not even dare to attack them close, while we beard him in his trenches every day ? Take my word for it, M. de la Noue, were there not a soldier in Rochelle, the women would be strong enough by themselves to keep off these Parisian butchers ! "

" Sir, the stronger party should speak moderately of his enemy ; and the weaker   "

" Who told you that we were the weaker ? " interrupted Laplace. " Does not God fight for us ? and was not Gideon, with three hundred men of Israel, too strong for all the host of the Midianites ? "

" You know, Master Mayor," continued La Noue, " better than any man, how insufficient are our stores. Powder is running low, and I have had to forbid the arquebusiers to risk long shots."

" Montgomery will send us some from England," said the mayor.

" The fire of heaven will fall on the Papists," said the minister.

" But bread grows dearer every day, Master Mayor."

" In a day or two the English fleet will be here, and then the town will have plenty."

" God will cause manna to fall, if it be needed ! " cried Laplace vehemently.

" As for the succour you speak of," went on La Noue, " a few days' southerly wind will make it impossible for it to enter the harbour. Besides, it may be taken."

" The wind will blow from the north. I prophesy it, O man of little faith ! " said the minister. " Thou hast lost thy courage at the same time as thy right arm ! "

La Noue seemed to have made up his mind to return him no answer. He went on, still addressing the mayor only :

" The loss of a single man falls heavier on us than the loss of ten on the enemy. I fear lest, if the Catholics press the siege with activity, we be forced to accept terms harder far than those which you have just scornfully rejected. And if, as I hope, the King deigns to content himself with having his authority recognized by the town, without demanding sacrifices which we cannot make, I believe it to be our duty to open our gates to him ; for after all, he is our master."

"We have no other master than Christ! And none but the impious can call Charles—the savage Ahab, who drinks the blood of the prophets—their master!" Thus cried the minister, whose rage seemed to redouble as he beheld La Noue's imperturbable calm.

"For my part," said the mayor, "I remember very well how, the last time the Admiral passed through our town, he said to us, ' The King has pledged me his word that all his subjects, Protestant and Catholic, shall be treated alike.' Six months later this same King, who pledged his word to the Admiral, had him murdered. If we open our gates, we shall have a Saint Bartholomew here as they had at Paris."

"The King was deceived by the Guises," said La Noue. " He repents it now, and would gladly make atonement for the bloodshed. If you provoke the Catholics by your obstinate refusal to treat, you will have to deal with all the forces of the kingdom, and the sole refuge of the reformed faith will be destroyed. Be persuaded by me, Master Mayor— peace! peace!"

"Coward!" cried the minister. "Thou desirest peace because thou fearest for thy life!"

" Oh, Master Laplace!" said the mayor.

" In short," went on La Noue coolly, " my last word is, that if the King will consent to put no garrison in La Rochelle, and to leave our meetings free, we ought to offer him the keys and assure him of our submission."

" Thou art a traitor!" said Laplace : "and thou hast been corrupted by the tyrants!"

"Good God! Master Laplace!" said the mayor again, "what are you saying?"

La Noue smiled slightly and contemptuously.

"You see, Master Mayor," said he, "the times we live in are strange: men of war speak of peace, and ministers preach war. My good sir," he continued, at last ad-

dressing Laplace, "it is dinner-time, I think, and your wife must be expecting you at home."

These last words put the finishing touch to the divine's fury. He could not hit on any verbal insult; and as a box on the ear is a good substitute for a reasonable answer, he dealt one on the old soldier's cheek.

"In God's name! what are you doing?" cried the mayor. "Strike M. de la Noue! the best citizen and the bravest soldier of Rochelle!"

Mergy, who was present, was about to administer to

Laplace a correction which he would not soon have forgotten, but La Noue held him back. For a single moment, when his grizzled beard was touched by the old madman's hand, there passed with the speed of thought over his eyes a flash of furious indignation. But his countenance at once recovered its impassive air. It might have been thought that the minister had struck the marble bust of a Roman senator, or that La Noue himself had been touched by some inanimate thing driven accidentally against him.

"Take the old man back to his wife," said he to one of the townsmen, who were dragging the minister away. "Tell her to have a care of him : he is surely not well to-day. And you, Master Mayor, I pray you have me ready a hundred and fifty citizen volunteers ; for I would make a sally to-morrow at break of day, just when the soldiers, who have spent the night in the trenches, are stiff with cold, like bears attacked at the thaw. I have often noticed that folk who have slept under a good roof have easy work at morning-tide with those who have passed the night in the open air. Monsieur de Mergy, if you are not in a great hurry for dinner, will you take a turn with me to the Gospel Bastion ? I should like to see how the enemy's works are getting on." Then, saluting the mayor, and resting his hand on the young man's shoulder, he bent his steps to the bastion.

They entered it the moment after two men had been mortally wounded by a gunshot ; the stones were dyed with blood, and one of the wretches was imploring his comrades to put him out of his misery. La Noue, his elbow on the parapet, gazed silently for some time at the besiegers' works ; then he turned towards Mergy. "All war is hideous," said he, "but a civil war ! That ball was rammed into a French cannon ; it was a Frenchman who levelled the gun, and held the match, and those whom the ball has killed are two Frenchmen. And yet, to cause death half a mile off is nothing ; but M. de Mergy, when one has to plunge a sword into the bosom of a man who cries for quarter in your own tongue . . . .! And we have done that very thing this very morning!"

"Ah, sir, but if you had seen the massacres on the twenty-fourth! If you had passed the Seine when it ran red, and

carried more corpses than it floats down iceblocks in winter when the frost breaks, you would feel little pity for those with whom we are fighting. To me every Papist is a murderer."

"Do not slander your country," said La Noue. "In yonder besieging army there are very few of the wretches of whom you speak. The soldiers are French peasants, who have quitted their ploughs to earn the King's pay : the gentlemen and the captains fight because of their oath of allegiance to the King. It may be that they are right and that we are rebels!"

"Rebels? But our cause is just : we fight for faith and life."

" I see you are not much troubled with scruples, M. de Mergy ; you are a happy warrior," and the old hero sighed deeply.

" By the Lord !" said a soldier, who had just let off his piece, " that devil there must bear a charmed life. I have been marking him down for three days, and I have never even grazed him."

" Whom do you mean ?" asked Mergy.

" There ! do you see the spark in the white doublet, with a red scarf and feather ? Every day he paces up and down, maugre our beards, as if to brave us. It is one of the gilt-swords of the Court, who came with Monsieur."

" It is a long shot," said Mergy ; " but never mind. Give me an arquebuss."

A soldier handed him his piece ; Mergy rested the end of the barrel on the parapet, and took a careful aim.

" Suppose he were a friend of yours ?" said La Noue. " Why do you want to play the musketeer thus ?"

Mergy, who was about to draw trigger, held his hand.

" I have no friends," he said, " but one, among the Catholics, and he, I am sure, is not among our besiegers."

" But suppose your brother were in Monsieur's suite, and it were he ?"

The arquebuss went off, but Mergy's finger had trembled, and the dust sent up by the bullet rose at some distance from the promenader. Mergy did not believe that his brother could be in the Catholic camp ; but he was not sorry to see that he had missed. The person at whom he had shot continued his slow walk, and at last disappeared behind one of the piles of fresh-heaped earth which were rising around the city on all sides.

CHAPTER XXVI.

THE SALLY.

"*Hamlet.* Dead for a ducat, dead!"
SHAKESPEARE.

A COLD drizzling rain, which had fallen uninterruptedly throughout the whole night, had just ceased when the dawning day was heralded in the sky by a pale light in the east. This light struggled through a heavy fog, which clung close

to the earth, though the wind dispersed it here and there,
making large gaps. But the grey fleecy masses soon
coalesced again, as the waves, cloven by a ship, fall back
and fill up the wake it has left. The champaign, covered
with this dense mist, through which tree-trunks peered at
intervals, looked like one great inundation.

In the town, the uncertain light of dawn, aided by the
flare of torches, shone upon a pretty numerous troop of
soldiers and volunteers, who were gathered in the street
leading to the Gospel Bastion. They were stamping their
feet on the pavement, and shuffling about without changing
their actual position, as men do who are pierced by the
damp and searching cold of a winter sunrise. They did not
spare oaths and vigorous execrations against the leader who
had put them under arms so early ; but despite the strength
of their language, there was to be detected in it the cheerful
hope which animates soldiers led by a chief whom they
value. They kept saying, in tones half-jesting and half-
angry, " This confounded Iron-arm, this Jack Never-sleep,
cannot eat his breakfast till he has beat up the quarters of
the babe-bolters yonder. A plague on him ! one never can
make sure of a night's rest with a devil of a fellow like
that. By our dead lord the Admiral's beard ! if I do not
hear the muskets talk soon, I shall go to sleep, as if I were
in bed. Thank God ! here is a dram coming to wake our
hearts in our bodies, and save us from catching cold in this
diabolical fog."

While the brandy was being served out to the soldiers, the
officers, clustering round La Noue, who was standing under
the penthouse of a shop, listened with interest to the
plan of the attack which he proposed to make on the besieging army. The roll of the drums was heard, each fell

into his place, and a minister came forward and blessed
the soldiers, exhorting them to do their duty, and promising
them eternal life if, for too good reasons, they were not
able to come back to the town and receive the rewards and
thanks of their fellow citizens. The sermon was a short
one; but La Noue thought it too long. He was not the
same man who the evening before deplored every drop of
French blood shed in the war; he was simply a soldier,
and seemed eager to revisit the scene of carnage. No
sooner was the minister's discourse finished; no sooner had
the soldiers returned their "Amen," than he cried in tones
firm and even harsh, "Comrades! the good man has said
well. Let us trust in God and our Lady of the Hardhitters!
I will kill the first man who fires before a Papist's stomach
is within range of his wad, if I come out alive myself!"

"Sir," whispered Mergy to him, "this is different talk from
last night's."

"Do you know Latin?" asked La Noue brusquely.

"Yes, sir," said Mergy.

"Then remember that admirable maxim, *Age quod agis.*"

He gave the signal. A cannon-shot was fired, and the
whole body set out at quick march for the open, while at
the same time small parties of soldiers, sallying by different
gates, went to beat up different parts of the hostile lines,
that the Catholics, thinking themselves assailed on all sides,
might not dare to send reinforcements to the scene of the
grand assault, for fear of deserting works which seemed
everywhere threatened.

The Gospel Bastion, against which the engineers of the
Catholic army had been concentrating their efforts, was
especially exposed to a battery of five guns, established on
a knoll, crowned by some ruined buildings, which had

before the siege been those of a mill. A ditch and an
earthwork guarded the approach to this from the city ; and
in front of the ditch several arquebusiers stood sentinel. But,
as the Protestant leader had foreseen, their guns, exposed
to the damp for several hours, were sure to be almost useless, and the attacking party, well equipped in all respects, and
ready for the assault, had a great advantage over men taken
by surprise, weary with watching, drenched with rain, and
shivering with cold. The first sentinels were despatched
with the cold steel, but some musket-shots, which had had the
luck to go off, woke the battery guards in time to see the
enemy already over the parapet, and climbing the ascent of
the mill-hill. Some resistance was attempted, but weapons
dropped from hands stiff with cold, and almost every arquebuss missed fire, while not a shot or blow of the assailants
was lost. Victory ceased to be doubtful, and already
the Protestants, masters of the battery, began to shout
savagely : " No quarter ! Remember the twenty-fourth of
August ! "

Some fifty soldiers with their captain occupied the mill-
tower ; and the officer, in his night garments, with a pillow
in one hand and his sword in the other, opened the gate
and came out, asking what the disturbance was. So far
was he from even thinking of a sally on the enemy's part,
that he fancied the noise to be due to some squabble among
his own soldiers. He was cruelly undeceived ; for a halberd-
blow stretched him on the ground bathed in his own blood.
His men had time to shut and barricade the gate of the
tower, and for some minutes they made good their defence
by firing from the windows. But there happened to be
stacked against the building a great mass of straw and
hay, as well as of brushwood for the gabions. The Pro-

testants set fire to this, and in a moment the flames had
enveloped the tower and climbed to its summit. Soon horrible cries came forth ; the roof had caught, and was ready
to fall on the wretches whom it had sheltered. The gate
was on fire, and the barricades they had made themselves
prevented their exit that way. If they attempted to jump
from the windows they fell into the burning pile or were
spitted on pike-points. Then was seen a hideous sight.
An ensign, sheathed in complete armour, tried, like the
rest, to leap from a narrow window. His corslet ended, as
was then a common enough fashion, in a sort of iron skirt [1]
covering the thighs and belly, and widening like a funnel-
mouth so as to give easy room for walking. The window
was not wide enough to let this part of the armour pass ;
and the ensign, in his excitement, had thrust himself so
violently in, that the greater part of his body was outside
without its being possible for him, held as he was in a sort
of vice, to move further. Meanwhile the flames rose to
him, heated his armour, and roasted him in it slowly as in a
furnace or in the famous brazen bull invented by [2] Phalaris.
The wretch uttered horrible cries, and vainly waved his
arms as if imploring succour. For a moment there was
silence among the attacking party ; then together, and as if
by common consent, they shouted a war-cry as though to
divert their own attention and drown the groans of the
burning man. He soon disappeared in a blast of flame and

[1] Armour like this can be seen at the Artillery Museum. A very fine
sketch of a tournament by Rubens shows how, notwithstanding this iron
skirt, it was still possible to mount a horse. The saddles have on them a
sort of small stool, which goes under the skirt and raises the rider till his
knees are almost on a level with his horse's head. For the man burnt in
his armour see D'Aubigné's " Histoire Universelle."

[2] " For," not " by," a slip of Mérimée's —*Translator's Note.*

smoke, and a helmet, red-hot and smoking, was seen to fall in the midst of the ruins of the tower.

In the heat of combat emotions of horror and grief last not long; the instinct of self-preservation speaks to the soldier's mind too forcibly for him to be able long to attend to the miseries of others. While some of the Rochellese pursued

the fugitives others spiked the guns, smashed their wheels, and hurled into the ditch the gabions of the battery and the corpses of its garrison.

Mergy, who had been one of the first in the escalade of the ditch and the rampart, took breath for a moment, just long enough to scratch the name of Diane on one of the

battery guns. Then he helped the others to destroy the
besiegers' works. Meanwhile a soldier had lifted up the
head of the Catholic captain, who gave no sign of life, while
another took his feet, and both swinging him between them
in cadence, were about to hurl him into the ditch. Suddenly
the apparent corpse, opening its eyes, recognized Mergy
and cried, "Quarter, Mergy! I am a prisoner, save me!
Do you not know your friend Béville?" The poor fellow's
face was covered with blood, and Mergy had some difficulty
in recognizing in this dying man the young courtier whom
he had left full of life and mirth. He had him stretched
carefully on the grass, himself bound up his wounds, and
after laying him across a horse, gave orders that he should
be taken gently into the town. In the act of bidding him
farewell and helping to lead the horse out of the battery,
he saw through an opening of the fog a body of cavalry
advancing at a trot, between the city and the mill. To all
appearance it was a detachment of Catholic troops trying to
cut off their retreat. Mergy at once hastened to warn
La Noue, and said, "If you will give me only two score
arquebusiers, I will throw myself behind the hollow way
through which they must pass, and if they do not turn tail
promptly I will give you leave to hang me!"

"Excellent, my boy!" said La Noue. "You will make a
good general some of these days. Come, men, follow this
gentleman and do what he tells you."

In a very short time Mergy had ensconced his arquebusiers along the hedge. He made them kneel on one
knee and get their weapons ready; but above all he forbade
a single shot to be fired till he gave the word. The hostile
cavalry rode rapidly up, and already their horse-hoofs were
clearly heard in the mud of the hollow way.

"Their captain," whispered Mergy, "is the red-plumed rascal whom we missed yesterday. Do not let us miss him to-day."

The arquebusier on his right nodded as though to say he would take care of that. The horsemen were not twenty paces off, and their leader, turning to his men, seemed about to give an order, when Mergy, rising suddenly, shouted "Fire!"

The captain with the red plume turned his head, and Mergy recognized his brother. He darted his hand towards his neighbour's piece to strike it aside; but before he touched it the shot sped. The horsemen, startled at the unexpected volley, fled in different directions over the plain; but Captain George fell pierced with two bullets.

CHAPTER XXVII.

THE HOSPITAL.

A FORMER monastery, sequestrated some time before by the Town Council of La Rochelle, had been, during the siege, turned into a hospital for the wounded. The pavement of the chapel (whence benches, altar, and all other furniture had been removed) was covered with hay and straw, and hither they carried the rank and file. The refectory was set apart for officers and gentlemen. It was a spacious apartment, handsomely panelled with old oak,

and its walls were pierced with wide pointed windows,
giving light enough for the surgical operations which unceasingly went on within it.

Here Captain George lay on a mattress, stained with his
own blood and with that of many other unfortunates who
had preceded him in this place of pain. A truss of straw
served him as pillow ; he was naked to the waist, for they
had just taken off his corslet and torn his shirt and doublet
open ; but his right arm still bore the steel armpiece and
gauntlet. A soldier was stanching the blood which flowed
from his wounds, one in the belly just below the cuirass,
the other, of less importance, in the left arm. Mergy was
so overwhelmed by grief that he was unable to be of any
effectual assistance. Now weeping on his knees in front of
the captain, now rolling on the ground with cries of despair,
he reproached himself unceasingly with having slain the
kindest of brothers and the best of friends. But the captain
was calm enough meanwhile and tried to moderate his
transports.

A few feet from his mattress was another on which the
luckless Béville lay in equally evil case. But his features
did not exhibit the same quiet resignation which was
noticeable on the captain's. From time to time he let slip
a muffled groan and turned his eyes to his neighbour as if
to beg a share of his own courage and fortitude.

A man of some forty years, dry, thin, bald, and covered
with wrinkles, entered the hall and drew near Captain
George, holding in his hand a green bag, whence there
issued a certain rattle very terrible to poor wounded men.
It was Master Brisart, a surgeon skilful enough for the
time, and a friend and pupil of the famous Ambrose Paré.
He had just operated ; for his arms were bare to the elbow.

and he was still girt with a large apron all stained with blood.

"Who are you, and what do you want with me?" asked George of him.

"I am a surgeon, my good sir, and if you do not know the name of Master Brisart, there must be many things of which you are ignorant. Come, pluck up a sheep's courage, as the saying is. I know something of gun-shot wounds, thank God! And I would I had as

many bags of a thousand livres each as I have extracted bullets from folks who are as hale to-day as I am myself."

"Well then, doctor, tell me the truth. The wound is mortal, if I know anything about it."

The surgeon examined the left arm first, and said, "A trifle!" Then he began to probe the other wound, a proceeding which soon forced the patient to grin horribly. He had strength enough left to push the doctor's hand away stoutly enough with his own right arm.

"No further, doctor, in God's name and the Devil's!" cried he. "I see by your face that my business is done."

"Well, sir, you see, I fear much that the bullet has crossed the small hypogastric intestine, and striking upwards has lodged in the spine, which we otherwise call in Greek, *rachis*. What makes me think so is that your legs are motionless and cold already—a pathological symptom which rarely deceives. In which case——"

"A gun-shot at point-blank and a ball in the spine! Plague on it, doctor, that is more than enough to lay one poor devil with his fathers. There, torture me no more, and let me die quietly."

"No! he shall live! He will live!" cried Mergy, fixing wild eyes on the surgeon and clutching his arm hard.

"Yes; he will live an hour longer—perhaps two, for he is a strong man," said Master Brisart coolly.

Mergy fell once more on his knees, seized the captain's right hand, and drenched the gauntlet which covered it, with tears.

"Two hours!" answered George. "So much the better: I feared I had longer to suffer."

"No! it is impossible!" cried Mergy sobbing. "George, you must not die. A brother cannot die by his brother's hand!"

"There, there, Bernard, calm yourself, and do not shake me so. I feel every motion of yours *here*. The pain is not too bad for the moment, if only it will last, as the fool said while he was falling from the steeple."

Mergy sat down by the mattress, his head resting on his knees and his face hidden by his hands. He did not move, and seemed stupefied: only now and then convulsive twitches made his whole body shake as though in the shivering fit of a fever, and groans unlike the sound of a human voice struggled from his breast.

As for the surgeon, after fixing a bandage or two merely to arrest the bleeding, he wiped his probe with great coolness.

" I should advise you strongly to set your affairs in order," he said. " If you want a minister, there are plenty here, and if you prefer a priest you can have one. I saw a monk just now, whom our people had taken prisoner. See, he is yonder, confessing that Popish officer who lies at the point of death."

" Give me something to drink," said the captain.

" Do nothing of the kind," replied the doctor, " or you will die an hour sooner."

" An hour of life is not worth a glass of wine. Come, good-bye, doctor ; my friend here at my side is waiting for you impatiently."

" Then shall I send you a minister or the monk ? "

" Neither one nor the other."

" What do you mean ? "

" Let me alone."

The surgeon shrugged his shoulders and turned to Béville.

" By my beard ! " cried he, " this is a beautiful wound ! These devils of volunteers strike like madmen ! "

" But I shall recover, shall I not ? " asked the wounded man feebly.

" Draw your breath," said Master Brisart.

Then they heard a sort of low whistle, produced by the air which left Béville's lungs by his wound as well as by his mouth, while the blood ran from the opening like crimson froth. The surgeon whistled himself, as if in echo of this strange sound ; and then he hastily bandaged the place, and without a word picked up his instrument-case and prepared to depart. Meanwhile Béville's eyes, glittering like torches, had followed all his movements.

"Well, doctor?" asked he, in trembling tones.

"Pack up your traps," said the surgeon coolly, as he turned away.

"Alas! to die so young!" cried the unhappy Béville, letting his head fall back on the straw which served him as pillow.

Captain George still asked for drink; but no one would give him so much as a glass of water, for fear of hastening his end—a singular kind of humanity, which serves only to prolong misery. At this moment La Noue, attended by Captain Dietrich and several other officers, entered the hall to visit the wounded. They all halted before George's mattress; and La Noue, leaning on his sword-hilt, looked from one brother to the other with eyes in which all the sympathy with which the sad scene inspired him was depicted. A flask slung at the German soldier's side attracted George's notice.

"Captain," said he, "you are an old soldier?"

"Yes; as a soldier I am old enough. The smoke of powder grizzles a man's beard faster than years. My name is Captain Dietrich Hornstein."

"Tell me, then," said George, "what you would do if you had my wound?"

Captain Dietrich considered the injuries for a moment, like a man accustomed to the sight and to judge their importance.

"I should put my conscience in order," answered he, "and then I should ask for a good glass of Rhenish, if there were a bottle anywhere about."

"Well, I only ask them for a glass of their wretched Rochelle wine, and the fools will not give it me."

Dietrich unslung his flask, which was of very goodly size, and made as though he would hand it to the wounded man.

"What are you doing, captain?" cried a musketeer. "The doctor says he will die at once if he drinks."

"What matter?" replied Dietrich; "he will at least have a little solace before death. Here, brave sir; I am only sorry not to have better wine to offer you."

"You are a gentleman, Captain Dietrich," said George, when he had drunk. Then handing the flask to his neighbour, "And you, my poor Béville, will you do me reason?"

But Béville shook his head and answered not.

"Ah! ah!" said George, "here comes more torment! What! will they never let me die in peace?"

He saw a minister coming forward, Bible under arm.

"My son," said the minister, "when you go———"

"Enough! enough!" answered George. "I know what you would say; but it is lost labour—I am a Catholic."

"A Catholic!" cried Béville. "Then you are a Free-thinker no longer?"

"But once," said the minister, "you were bred in the reformed faith; and at this solemn and terrible moment, when you are about to appear before the supreme Judge of deeds and of consciences———"

"I am a Catholic! By the devil's horns! leave me alone!"

"But———"

"Captain Dietrich," said George, "will you not take pity on me? You have done me one great service; I beg you do me yet another. See that I am allowed to die without preachments and jeremiads."

"You had better withdraw," said the captain to the minister. "You see he is in no mood to listen to you."

La Noue beckoned to the monk, who at once approached.

" Here is a priest of your own religion," said La Noue to Captain George. " We make no pretensions to force men's consciences."

" Monk or minister, let them all go to the devil!" answered the wounded man.

But the two divines stood on each side of his bed, and seemed ready to fight for the dying patient.

" This gentleman is a Catholic," said the monk.

" But he was born a Protestant," said the minister ; " he belongs to me."

" He was converted," said the one.

" But he wishes to die in the faith of his fathers," retorted the other.

" Confess, my son."

" Repeat your Creed, my son."

" Do you not die a good Catholic ? " asked the monk.

" Take away this messenger of Antichrist!" cried the minister, feeling that the majority of the audience was on his side ; and immediately a zealous Huguenot soldier grasped the monk by his girdle, and thrust him back, crying —

" Hence, shaveling gallows-bird! 'tis long since mass has ceased to be said at Rochelle ! "

" Hold, there ! " said La Noue.   " If this gentleman wishes to confess himself, I pledge my word that none shall interfere."

" Very many thanks, M. de la Noue," said the dying man faintly.

" You are all witnesses," interrupted the monk, " he wishes to confess ! "

" No ! may the devil take me, no ! "

"He returns to the faith of his ancestors!" cried the minister.

"No! A thousand thunders! Leave me, both of you! Am I dead already, that the ravens are quarrelling over my carcass? I will have neither your mass nor your psalms."

"He blasphemes!" cried in unison the two ministers of the rival faiths.

"It is well to believe in something," observed Captain Dietrich with unruffled calmness.

"I believe," said George; "I believe that you are a good fellow who will deliver me from these harpies. There! get away with you both, and let me die like a dog."

"Yea! die like a dog!" said the minister, turning away in a rage. The monk crossed himself, and drew near Béville's couch, while La Noue and Mergy held the Protestant divine back. "Make one more effort!" said Mergy. "Pity him, pity me!"

"Sir," said La Noue to the dying man, "take an old soldier's word for it, the exhortations of a servant of God can soothe dying hours. Do not hearken to the counsels of a guilty vanity, and do not lose your soul out of idle bravado."

"Sir," replied the captain, "I have not thought of death to-day for the first time. I need no one's exhortations to prepare for it. I never loved bravado, and I love it now less than ever. But in the devil's name, I will have nothing to do with their nonsense." The minister shrugged his shoulders, and La Noue sighed. Both departed slowly and with bowed heads.

"Comrade," said Dietrich, "you must be in the devil's own pain to speak as you do."

"Yes, captain. I am."

" Then I hope that the good God will not be offended at
your words, though they sound desperately like blasphemy.
With a gun-shot right through the body, confound it, one
may swear a little to keep one's heart up."

George smiled and took the flask once more. " Your
health, captain ! You are the best nurse a wounded soldier
can have," and as he spoke he held out his hand. Dietrich
clasped it, not without certain signs of emotion. " The
devil !" he murmured to himself, "suppose my brother
Hennig were a Catholic, and I had shot him through the
body ! This, then, was what Mila's prophecy meant."

" George, my friend," said Béville in a piteous tone,
" speak to me once ! We are going to die. 'Tis a terrible
moment. Are you still minded as you used to be when you
converted me to Atheism ?"

" Of course I am. Take courage ; in a minute or two our
sufferings will be over."

" But this monk tells me of flames—of devils—of all
sorts of things. Meseems all this is not comforting."

" Nonsense !"

" But suppose it were all true ?"

" Captain," said George, " I bequeath to you my corslet
and my sword ; and I would I had something better to offer
you for the good wine you have given me so kindly."

" George, my friend," began Béville once more, " it would
be terrible if what he says were true . . . . eternity !"

" You poltroon !"

" Yes, it is very easy to say 'poltroon,' but poltroonery is
allowable when it is a case of suffering everlastingly."

" Well then, confess yourself."

" But—but—I pray you tell me, are you *sure* there is no
hell ?"

" Bah ! "

" Nay, but answer. Are you *sure?* Give me your word that there is none."

" I am sure of nothing. If there be a devil, we shall see whether he is as black as they paint him."

" What ! You are *not* sure ? "

" Confess, confess, I tell you."

" But you will laugh at me ? "

The captain could not repress a smile, but then he said in a serious tone, " If I were in your place I should make confession ; for it is the safest game after all, and once shriven and anointed, one is ready for anything."

" Well, I will do as you do. Confess yourself first."

" Not I."

" Faith, then, you may say what you like, I will die a good Catholic. Come, father, hear me say my *confiteor*, and prompt me a little, for I have half forgotten it."

As he confessed himself Captain George drank another sip of wine, stretched his head on his uneasy pillow, and shut his eyes, remaining quiet for some quarter of an hour. Then he clenched his lips and shuddered as he gave vent to a long groan, wrenched from him by pain. Mergy, thinking him dying, uttered a cry and lifted his head. But the captain opened his eyes.

" What, again ?" said he gently, pushing him back. " Pray, Bernard, be calm."

" George ! George ! and you are dying by my hand !"

" What then ? I am not the first Frenchman killed by a brother, and I do not think I shall be the last. Besides, I have none but myself to blame. When Monsieur, after delivering me from prison, took me with him, I swore that I would never draw sword. But they told me that this poor fellow Béville was attacked, and when I heard the firing, I took a fancy to see the thing too close."

He shut his eyes again, but opened them once more to say to Mergy, " Madame de Turgis bade me tell you that she loves you still." And he smiled kindly.

These were his last words, and he died some quarter of an hour later without seeming to suffer much. In a minute or two Béville expired in the arms of the monk, who afterwards assured his hearers that he had distinctly heard in the air the joyful cries of the angels who received the soul of this repentant sinner, while the devils returned a howl of triumph from underground as they carried off the spirit of Captain George.

It may be seen in any history of France how La Noue, sick of civil war, and tormented by his conscience with reproaches for fighting against his King, quitted Rochelle ; how the Catholic army was forced to raise the siege ; and how the fourth peace was soon followed by the death of Charles IX.

But did Mergy console himself? And did Diane take another lover? I leave these questions to the decision of the reader, who can thus in every case suit the conclusion of the story to his own taste.

CHISWICK PRESS:—C. WHITTINGHAM AND CO., TOOKS COURT,
CHANCERY LANE, LONDON.

ImTheStory.com

SD - #0020 - 260123 - C0 - 229/152/20 - PB - 9781314906080 - Gloss Lamination